A Career in Law
THE WAY IN

Fourth Edition

Brian Heap
Director
Higher Education Advice and
Planning Service

HLT Publications

HLT PUBLICATIONS
200 Greyhound Road, London W14 9RY

First Published 1990
Revised Edition 1991
Third Edition 1992
Fourth Edition 1994

ISBN 0 7510 0436 7

British Library Cataloguing-in-Publication.

A CIP Catalogue record for this book is available from the
British Library.

Printed and bound in Great Britain.

CONTENTS

CONTENTS

ACKNOWLEDGEMENTS

I would like to thank the Law Society for providing information covering the training of Solicitors, UCAS for advising on their application systems and Mr Jason Tarsh of the Department for Education for allowing me to publish statistics on graduate employment. I also wish to thank the University of Bristol for the use of extracts from their prospectus.

Brian Heap

1 INTRODUCTION

'Law is the cement of society and also an essential medium of change. A knowledge of law increases one's understanding of public affairs. Its study promotes accuracy of expression, facility in argument and skill in interpreting the written word, as well as some understanding of social values. Its practice does, of course, call for much routine, careful and unexciting work and it is for you to decide whether you think you are temperamentally suited to it.'

This extract is taken from that excellent little book *Learning the Law* by Glanville Williams (Stevens and Sons) which should be essential reading for anyone contemplating the study of Law at a university or college or as a professional qualification.

No law case, however, can ever proceed without very careful preparation and similarly no student should ever make the decision to follow such a demanding course of study – or any course of study – without being fully aware of what is involved and without careful planning.

At a recent interview for a place in Law at Oxford, one applicant proclaimed that he had wanted to be a lawyer since he was eight years of age! There may have been other reasons for his rejection, but an opinion concerning a career in law as seen on TV, with a clever criminal lawyer manipulating a jury, is no more a true reflection of the extent of the career than the work of a brain or heart surgeon is to a career in medicine.

No solicitor or barrister would ever jump to conclusions on the basis of superficial evidence and no intending law student should be attracted to the career simply because of its status and high salaries, as is often the case. Let us be equally professional therefore and proceed to explore what a career in law really involves, what courses are available and how to prepare a successful application.

2 STUDYING LAW

Studying law not only provides a means of entering the legal profession, but is also a stimulating and rewarding academic exercise. The development of logical thought and methodical preparation of argument is something that is of value in any career that you may choose to follow.

As a lawyer, you will need to master the detail of the law, together with the ability to present this knowledge in a rational and decisive way.

In addition to acquiring a general knowledge of the English Legal System, the student will also study what are known as the 'core subjects'. These are Constitutional Law, Contract Law, Criminal Law, Tort, Land Law and the Law of Trusts. Most institutions allow students to supplement these basic subjects with additional options in a variety of other legal specialities. However, do remember that if you are intending to go on to become a barrister or a solicitor you must ensure that you do cover these 'core subjects' to keep your qualifying period to a minimum.

Sources of English Law

England is a democracy, and as such depends heavily upon Parliament for the creation of law. However, England is also a common law jurisdiction, which means that many legal principles are found by reference to earlier cases. Our membership of the European Community has also introduced aspects of EC law into our legal system and a knowledge of this area of law is essential.

Your studies will familiarise you with the techniques necessary to interpret legislation, ascertain the essential principles in a case, and discover the applicability of European law.

Statutory Interpretation

The traditional view that Parliament is sovereign, and can therefore legislate as it sees fit, is subject now to the effect of EC law. Nevertheless, Parliament may make new laws, bringing about great political and social changes, and it may alter, simplify, or improve or repeal existing laws. The judges must apply the law made by Parliament; they are not free to ignore or alter it. In order to apply the law, they must interpret the statute. In doing this they will adopt one of a number of approaches; namely the literal rule, the golden rule and the mischief rule or purposive approach.

The literal rule requires the judge to give the words in the statute their literal meaning even if the result is undesirable. If, however, the result becomes manifestly absurd or repugnant, judges may vary the meaning of the words to avoid the absurdity or repugnance. This is called the golden rule.

In most cases, though, the words of a statute are capable of bearing more than one meaning, and a decision must then be taken to decide which meaning Parliament intended. To assist them, judges will use the mischief rule or purposive approach, which requires them to consider what mischief or defect Parliament was trying to correct, or what purpose the statute was designed to serve.

In addition there are grammatical rules of construction (all with impossible Latin names!) and presumptions to assist in ascertaining the meaning of words in a statute.

Judicial Precedent

As well as being confined by statute law, judges must also follow certain earlier judicial decisions. This doctrine of binding judicial precedent, or *stare decisis,* is vital to an understanding of the law. It should ensure that there is certainty, uniformity and consistency. It can, however, lead to inflexibility and injustice.

In the course of your studies you will develop the ability to define the essential binding part of the judgment, called the *ratio decidendi.* The rest of the judgment is termed *obiter dicta* and may be used as guidance in the future. It is possible to avoid being bound by an earlier decision if one can distinguish the facts of the case from that which fails to be considered. You must, however, be careful not to 'distinguish the indistinguishable'!

Civil and Criminal Law

The English legal system makes a distinction between civil and criminal law. The criminal law is concerned with wrongs that not only affect 'the victim' but which are of a nature that society has an interest in preventing and punishing them. The civil law is also concerned with wrongs, but the nature of the wrong is such that it is left to the aggrieved individual to bring an action. We sometimes refer to the civil law as being a way of recognising rights.

In criminal cases we talk of a prosecution being taken against the defendant, and the result of the case is referred to as a conviction or acquittal. If there is a conviction the defendant will be punished, for example, by a fine or imprisonment. Whereas in civil cases the person who institutes the action, or sues, is referred to as the plaintiff, and the person against whom the action lies is referred to as the defendant. The result of a civil case is called judgment for the plaintiff or defendant, and usually compensation is awarded.

Civil and criminal cases take place in different courts and different procedural rules apply. Cases in civil courts are known by the names of the parties: *Smith v Bloggs* (pronounced Smith and Bloggs). In criminal cases the prosecution is usually brought in the name of the Queen, and would be written as *Reg.* or *R v Smith* (pronounced as the Queen against Smith, or informally R v Smith).

The Court Structure

The distinction between civil and criminal law is reflected in the court structure. While several courts have jurisdiction over both civil and criminal cases, civil cases are dealt with by a different system of courts dealing with criminal cases. What follows is a basic outline of the two court structures.

Civil court structure

The Magistrates' and County Courts are at the entry level to the civil system, along with a number of specialist tribunals, eg Social Security Appeals, Industrial and Rent Tribunals. At the next level are the Crown Court (in its civil jurisdiction) and the Employment Appeals Tribunal. Above is the High Court which has three main divisions: Family; Queen's Bench (including the Admiralty and Commercial Courts); and Chancery. The Court of Appeal (Civil Division) is the first appellate court; the second – and highest – appellate court for civil cases is the House of Lords.

Criminal court structure

The Magistrates' Courts are the starting point for all criminal cases, and on the next tier is the Crown Court. The Queen's Bench Divisional Court hears appeals from the Magistrates' Courts, both direct and via the Crown Court. The Criminal Division of the Court of Appeal comes next in the hierarchy and again the House of Lords is the final appellate court.

Role of the European Court of Justice

Any court may refer a point of European law to the European Court of Justice for decision (this is not an appeal).

Personnel of the Law

The judges who preside over the courts are selected from the ranks of practising lawyers. The higher the court, the more senior the judge. The Lord Chancellor is responsible for advising the Government and the Queen on the appointment of judges.

The judges of the House of Lords are called Lords of Appeal in Ordinary, and judges in the Court of Appeal are called Lord Justices of Appeal. High Court judges are referred to as puisne (pronounced 'puny', and from the old French for 'junior' or 'inferior') judges, whilst circuit judges sit in the County Courts and Crown Court.

In the Magistrates' Court, decisions are made by lay people, called Justices of the Peace, or by a stipendiary magistrate who is legally qualified. The professional lawyers who present cases in court are usually barristers, although cases in the lower courts may be presented by solicitors. Solicitors tend to give general advice and assistance to their clients, referring cases to barristers for more specialist advice and advocacy.

3 A CAREER AS A SOLICITOR (ENGLAND AND WALES)

At the present time there are about 50,000 solicitors in practice in the UK (compared with 6,000 barristers, 2,000 judges and 29,000 magistrates). The great majority of solicitors work in private practice with about 5,000 being employed by commercial and industrial organisations and 3,000 in local government work.

A solicitor in private practice usually starts as an assistant solicitor, later becoming a partner and sharing the profits and management of the business. Firms of solicitors vary from large partnerships in the City of London and other large towns to smaller 'High Street' practices throughout England and Wales.

Private Practice

The role of the solicitor in practice is to give legal advice and to counsel their clients on the best way to proceed with their particular problem. Much of the work is quite routine in nature and articled clerks or other clerks (legal executives) often assist in these duties.

A large proportion of a 'High Street' solicitor's work will be involved with conveyancing property – the purchase of houses, flats, shops, even factories! Anyone purchasing property needs to have safeguards against any future plans for the development or otherwise of the land on which the property is situated and also needs advice on the contract of sale, etc.

Solicitors also advise clients on the course of action to take if they are facing criminal charges – anything in fact from a traffic offence to murder – since many such cases need to be defended in a court of law.

The drafting of wills is yet another side of the solicitor's work and he or she may also be responsible to see that the terms of the will are executed (by acting as an executor or administrator). Compensation claims, divorce, custody of children, and maintenance also fall within the province of the law in addition to anything from the setting up of companies to debt collecting.

In small town practices, many clients will use the same firm throughout their lives, but at the other end of the spectrum large city practices may concentrate on one particular specialism such as company law, shipping, airline or commercial law, or libel and slander (defamation).

If you have a hidden talent, therefore, for drafting important documents then there could be a place for you; alternatively as a solicitor you might prefer court work (litigation), conducting cases in magistrates' or county courts.

Civil Service

Outside private practice there are still very many opportunities to practise law – the Civil Service being one of them.

Large numbers of lawyers (solicitors and barristers) work for the government legal service in almost all departments. Civil Service departments are constantly needing to review their policies (economic and political) and legal experts are in constant demand. These departments include:

Agriculture, Fisheries and Food which includes the EC common agricultural policy;

Education and Science – from nursery school to universities – involving pay scales, the youth service and school meals service;

Energy – coal, gas, oil, electricity and nuclear power;

Employment – covering all aspects of manpower;

Environmental and Transport – involving housing, planning, road construction and transport;

Health and Social Security – administering the National Health Services;

Trade and Industry – EC policy, exports and imports;

The Ministry of Defence – formulating defence policy and administering the armed services.

There are also other departments such as HM Treasury (economic policy); the Cabinet Office (administering Cabinet business); the Central Office of Information; the Foreign and Commonwealth Office (British interests abroad) and the Home Office (law and order and justice). Another important legal area is that of the Lord Chancellor's Department which administers all criminal and civil courts (except magistrates' courts) in England and Wales.

Other departments include the Land Registry, Inland Revenue, the Office of Fair Trading, the Health and Safety Executive, HM Customs and Excise, the Crown Estate Office, the Charity Commission, the Department of Public Prosecutions, the Public Record Office, Ordnance Survey, National Savings and Stationery Office.

There are, however, other opportunities for work as a solicitor, for example in local government within departments of education, town and country planning, and social services. In such a role much of your time will be spent arranging for the election of council members to carry out their duties.

Alternatively, you may be amongst the 5,000 solicitors in commerce or industry since most large companies now have their own legal departments dealing with business law, company law, taxation and other specialised areas.

The role of a solicitor therefore is to provide clients with skilled legal advice in private practice, in local or central government, the Magistrates Courts Service or a commercial or industrial organisation. The work of a solicitor varies as widely as the community they serve, covering business affairs, commercial property, residential conveyancing, family work, probate and wills, personal injury, crime and many other legal problems.

Have You the Right Qualities to be a Solicitor?

A recent report from the Law Society stated that:

'The Dickensian image of a solicitor as a middle-class, elderly man has changed quite considerably. Solicitors these days come from both sexes, all races, and from any social background. The profession is "getting younger" too – about half of all practising solicitors these days are under 36 and only a minority of solicitors qualifying now have family connections with the legal profession. It is no coincidence that many well-known figures have made it to the very top in government, commerce and industry after qualifying as solicitors.'

But what qualities do you need?

a) Have you a good memory?
b) Are you numerate?
c) Have you a good command of language?
d) Have you the ability to get to grips with a problem?
e) Have you high personal standards of integrity?
f) Have you the ability to communicate with others at all levels – and to listen to them?
g) Have you the patience to cope with routine matters?
h) Have you a cool head when the pressure is on?
i) Have you common sense?

Qualifying to be a Solicitor

The majority of newly qualified solicitors have taken a degree in law or another subject and this is the recommended route.

Law Graduates

About 75 per cent of solicitors qualify by way of a law degree which is the quickest and most common way to qualify as a solicitor. It involves studying for a qualifying law degree and then proceeding direct to the Legal Practice Course, which is the professional training for solicitors.

In order to be a qualifying law degree, the course should contain the following six 'core' subjects:

Contract • Land Law • Equity and Trusts • Tort • Criminal Law • Constitutional and Administrative Law

In order to be accepted for a qualifying law degree, it is usually necessary to have very good 'A' level grades (or their equivalent). You can study any subject at 'A' level; the important thing is that the subjects you study are academic, eg English, history, sciences, etc, rather than 'vocational' (eg photography, surveying, etc) and that you do well in them. Science 'A' levels are normally just as acceptable as arts subjects and no one subject is essential for admission to a law degree course. For further information about entry qualifications, you should contact the institutions of your choice direct. You should always check to ensure that the six 'core' subjects are covered.

Following your law degree you will then take a one year Legal Practice Course.

In May 1990 the Council of the Law Society approved in principle the Training Committee's report 'Training Tomorrow's Solicitors'. The report proposed that the Law Society's Final Course for solicitors should be replaced from September 1993 by a more practical Legal Practice Course. The course would be taught and assessed by approved institutions subject to the Society's supervision exercised through the Legal Practice Course Board. The Board would also be responsible for monitoring the quality of the course.

Course Format and Assessment

The purpose of the course is to ensure that trainee solicitors entering training contracts have the necessary knowledge and skills to undertake appropriate tasks under proper supervision during the contract. A full-time Legal Practice Course will run for one academic year; a part-time course for two years. The introduction of part-time courses will increase the flexibility of the training scheme and access to the profession.

The curriculum of the Legal Practice Course comprises:

a)   *The Compulsory Areas*

Conveyancing
Wills, Probate and Administration
Business Law and Practice
Litigation and Advocacy

All four areas will combine substantive law, procedure and practical skills work.

b)   *Optional Subjects*

Students will be required to study two optional courses from a range covering subjects of interest in 'private client' and 'corporate client' work. It is open to practitioners and other groups to suggest to the Board areas of law for inclusion as optional courses and these will be communicated to the teaching institution on a regular basis.

c)   *Pervasive Topics*

Certain topics have been identified as of such importance that they should be assessed through the compulsory areas. These topics include:

Professional Conduct
Investment Business under the Financial Services Act
European Community Law
Revenue Law

d)   *Practical Skills*

The course will seek to develop certain essential skills including:

Practical Legal Research
Drafting
Interviewing
Negotiating and Advocacy

Legal Practice Courses are validated and organised by the following institutions: the Colleges of Law at Chester, Stone Street, Guildford and York. (Further details are obtainable from the Registrar, College of Law, Braboeuf Manor, St Catherines, Guildford, Surrey GU3 1HA), and at the following universities: University of Central England, Nottingham Trent University, the University of Northumbria at Newcastle, the University of the West of England, Bristol, De Montfort University, Leicester, Birmingham University, London Guildhall University, Manchester Metropolitan University, the University of Wolverhampton, Leeds Metropolitan University, the University of Glamorgan, Huddersfield University, the University of Westminster and the Cardiff Law School (Museum Avenue, Cardiff CF1 1XD). Details of these universities appear in Chapter 12.

Application forms for the Legal Practice Course can be obtained from the Legal Practice Course Central Applications Board, Admail 44, London SW1P 1YL.

After completing the Legal Practice Course it is then necessary to undertake a two-year training contract.

In order to find a suitable employer many firms will visit the university or college where you are studying to talk about training with them. Each year the Law Society runs a Careers and Recruitment Fair to enable employers and students to meet and discuss opportunities in the professions.

In order to find out which firms and organisations offer training, you should consult a book called ROSET (Register of Solicitors Employing Trainees) which is available from the university or college library or from the Law Society. It is published by the Law Society and lists all firms and organisations employing trainee solicitors by region and by specialism so you can find the firm offering the kind of work you want to do in the area you want to live. Many firms offer training two years in advance but they tend to be the larger organisations and if you wish to work for a smaller firm or, for example, a local authority, you often need to apply nearer the time. From 1994 firms and organisations which offer training have to be authorised by the Law Society which also interviews trainees and employers to ensure that the training is of the appropriate standard. Most people train in private practice, but you can also train in local government, the Crown Prosecution Service and the Magistrates' Courts Service. There are also opportunities to train in central government, commerce and industry.

Non-law Graduates

If you prefer to take a degree in a subject other than law, this is perfectly acceptable, but qualification will take longer. Having been awarded your degree you then complete the Academic Stage of Training by means of the Common Professional Examination or recognised alternative.

The Common Professional Examination is taken after a one-year full-time or a two-year part-time course covering the six core subjects. Courses are offered by a range of institutions, though Holborn College is unique in offering the only part-time course available on Saturdays.

Some institutions offer a part-time or full-time Diploma in Law Course recognised for entry to the Legal Practice Course, but not for entry to the Bar examinations. Here you would cover the six 'core' subjects and some additional legal topics.

A small number of institutions including Holborn College offer two-year post-graduate law degree courses which cover the six 'core' subjects and other legal studies.

After successful completion of the academic stage of training by the Common Professional Examination or an alternative, you then proceed to the Legal Practice Course, followed by the two-year training contract. It is possible for those who have taken the CPE to complete the training contract before the Legal Practice Course, if the employer agrees.

The Non-Graduate Route

If you have four GCSEs (waived for those over 25) you can become a student member of the Institute of Legal Executives and train to be a legal executive. This involves obtaining a training post as a trainee legal executive with a firm of solicitors or similar organisation, joining the Institute of Legal Executives and undertaking the Institute's Part I and Part II examinations. This normally takes between three and four years. If possible, you should study for three of the six 'core' subjects of law (see above).

After passing the Part II Examination you will become a Member of the Institute of Legal Executives. You must have served five years (two after membership) in a legal office and be 25 years of age before you become eligible to become a Fellow of the Institute of Legal Executives. During this time, you should undertake the remaining 'core' subjects as Diploma examinations via the Institute.

As a Fellow of the Institute of Legal Executives, having passed the six 'core' subjects of law, it is then possible to enrol as a student member of the Law Society and attend the Legal Practice Course. If you have been in continuous legal employment, the requirement to serve a Training Contract (below) may be waived, but you would have to complete the Professional Skills Course, after completing the Legal Practice Course.

If you wish to pursue this route, you should contact the Institute of Legal Executives whose address is Kempston Manor, Kempston, Bedford MK42 7AB.

Mature Students

Some people decide to train as a solicitor at a later stage in their careers. To do so you must be over 25 years of age to enrol with the Law Society. You will need to satisfy the Society that a minimum standard of education has been attained and that you can show exceptional ability in business, academic, professional or administrative work. Like non-law graduates the Common Professional Examination must be taken, but over a two-year (not a one-year) period. The Legal Practice Course must also be taken and then you will serve two years training as an articled clerk. (Students or others working in the legal profession may gain exemptions from some of the examinations to be taken.)

The Training Contract

You will enter a two-year training contract with your chosen employer. You will be offered training in at least three different areas of law, taken from a list laid down by the Law Society. The type of work offered will depend very much on the employer you train with. It may include matters such as landlord and tenant work, tax work, probate and wills work, matrimonial law, civil litigation, planning work or crime. Some firms only offer commercial work, others concentrate on private client work and some may offer a mixture. If your training contract starts in 1994, you will be required to take the Professional Skills Course which will cover the areas of accounts, investment business, personal work management, professional conduct and advocacy. The course will last for up to 20 days, and will be offered by a number of organisations in a variety of ways. It may be possible to study for the course by distance learning, so that the modules can be covered at an appropriate time in your training. Some firms may offer the course 'in-house'.

You will have to consider which type of work interests you before you decide where to apply for training. A large number of firms offer general experience, but others are more specialised, so you will need to find out about the type of work available before you apply.

The structure of your training will also depend upon the type of firm you choose. Wherever you train you will work in at least three, but usually four or five different areas of the law over the two-year period. Most firms are divided into departments, each dealing with a particular area of the law, and you will spend up to six months working in each chosen department. You will learn practical skills such as drafting documents, advocacy and interviewing clients. Your work will be closely supervised and regularly reviewed but as the training progresses, the responsibility you are given will increase.

At the end of your training contract you may apply for admission as a solicitor. The law is continually changing, and solicitors are required to undertake continuing education as long as they practise.

School Leavers (very few pupils decide to qualify in this way)

All school leavers must first apply to the Law Society for an enrolment certificate and they must have achieved a minimum standard of education. The requirements are:

a) Four GCE passes or GCSE (Grades A, B or C), including three 'A' Levels; or
b) Five GCE passes or GCSE (Grades A, B or C), including two 'A' Levels; or
c) Six GCE passes or GCSE (Grades A, B or C), including two 'A' Levels and two 'AS' Levels.

There is also a minimum points system in operation. The table below should be used to calculate the points required at 'A' Level and 'AS' Level.

GRADE	'A' LEVEL POINTS	'AS' LEVEL POINTS
A	10	5
B	8	4
C	6	3
D	4	2
E	2	1

The minimum points required are as follows:

> 14 points from two 'A' Level subjects taken at one sitting.

> 18 points from three 'A' Level subjects or two 'A' Level and two 'AS' Level subjects taken at one sitting.

> 20 points from three 'A' Level or two 'A' Level and two 'AS' Level subjects taken at not more than two sittings.

> ('AS' Level subjects may not be taken into account when calculating points unless a minimum of two 'A' Levels is held. Equivalent qualifications will be considered in lieu of the above.)

School leavers then take a one-year course at a university or college in four law subjects in the first half of an examination known as the Solicitors' First Examination. (Only a limited number of places is available for this examination.)

Five years must then be spent as an articled clerk. During this time, part-time study must be done for a further four law subjects, making up the second half of the Solicitors' First Examination (it is usual for two subjects to be taken after the first year and two after the second).

After completing the Solicitor's First Examination, you must attend a one-year course studying for the Law Society's Final Examination, but the time you spend on the course will count as part of your training as an articled clerk. When you have completed your training in articles and you have passed the final exams, you may be admitted as a solicitor.

Further Reading

A Career in Law, B A Hogan, Sweet and Maxwell (1981).
Before you see a Solicitor, Gerald Sanctuary, Oyez Publishing (1983).
How to Study Law, A Bradney, V Fisher and others, Sweet and Maxwell (1986).
Learning the Law, Glanville Williams, Stevens (1945: 11th edition 1982).
Which Firm of Solicitors? John Pritchard, Legalease Limited (1987).

Further details can be obtained from the Law Society (address all enquiries to 'Careers Information'), 113 Chancery Lane, London WC2A 1PL.

Financial Support for Students taking the CPE or the Legal Practice Course

Local Authority Grants

Information

Your Local Authority will issue a leaflet or booklet including details of mandatory and discretionary award policies, with reference to courses which the authority will consider for the purposes of financial support.

Both the CPE and the Legal Practice Courses fall into the category of discretionary awards, which means that the authority will decide, using a series of criteria, whether an individual will qualify for an award.

Often, since they are dependent largely on local funds, discretionary funds are very limited and you should apply immediately after the first date published for the receipt of applications, usually later than the date for applications for mandatory awards. (The dates differ, so check with your Local Authority.)

More general guidance on grants is provided in the Department for Education booklet 'Grants to Students – A Brief Guide' and can be obtained from careers and appointment libraries of Higher Education Institutions, large reference libraries and the Department for Education.

Applications Procedure

Many enquiries for grant support for CPE and LPC are discouraged by telephone. If you want your application to be properly considered, *you must complete a form*, providing details of your education, your circumstances, your income and savings, and if appropriate, information about your parents' or spouse's income.

If your grant is to be calculated on your parents' or spouse's income, allowances are made for their expenditure and an amount called *residual income* is calculated in order to determine the contribution that would be made, which is aggregated to the total amount payable to you.

Mature and Independent Status

Your own income over the past three years or more will also have a bearing on whether you qualify and, if you qualify, the amount you will receive.

Mature entry and independent status considerations are complex and vary from one Local Authority to another, so you should read the guidelines carefully before you apply.

Often, a 'mature' candidate will be over 23 or 25, but sometimes the age will be determined at 20 or 27. Some authorities have no mature entry criteria at all and will award a grant only to someone *below* a certain age, eg 25. The need to make extensive and detailed enquiries is, therefore, of paramount importance.

Applying

As sources of finance for further study are limited and Local Authorities continue to receive ever-increasing applications for support, the level of competition between candidates for awards increases.

Careful preparation of your initial grant application is important. You might use academic and character references, enlist the support of someone in the legal profession of good standing in your local area, or a local MP. If you feel your application has not been given proper consideration, if you have been refused and you feel the decision contravened any of the regulations or you were not given adequate explanation for the reasons for refusal, you should enquire about appeal and write to the Authority's own Chief Executive Officer to explain the circumstances.

Career Development Loans

These loans are operated on behalf of the Department of Employment by three banks: Barclays, The Clydesdale and the Co-operative. They are available to pay for vocational courses (up to 80 per cent of the course fee) and may also include payments for living expenses where the course is full-time. The minimum loan is £300 and the maximum is £5,000. The interest on the loan is paid by the Government during the course and up to three months afterwards. Thereafter the trainee pays back the loan at a rate of interest agreed with the bank. The conditions include that the applicant is not receiving any Government grant or help from an employer. An information booklet including an application form may be obtained from Job Centres and participating bank branches. See also bibliography.

Charities and Grant-Making Trusts

Your Local Authority Awards Officer will also have information about local charities and any grant-making trust for which you may qualify. There will be a charities register which can be considered in order to advise you, which may be available in the local reference library. Qualifications for these awards vary enormously and they are often so specific that your eligibility will be limited to a very few. Usually they provide for the award of small amounts of money only and should not be relied upon to provide financial support for either tuition or maintenance for a whole year.

Law Society Bursary Scheme

The Law Society has a limited bursary scheme, a variety of funds and grant-making trusts providing grants and loans which have been grouped together into an umbrella scheme. The fund in total is very limited and there are both competitive elements and hardship criteria which must be applied. For example, a candidate needs to be both outstanding in achievement or education, and genuinely in need of support, with no other access to major funding via own, parents' or spouse's income or a local authority award, in order to be considered.

Application forms are provided from 1 March to 30 April in the year in which the applicant hopes to commence his or her course. Further information can be obtained from the Law Society Legal Education Department by writing or telephoning as indicated. The closing date is 10 May; this date is rigidly applied.

Sponsorship

An increasing number of firms will sponsor students, mainly those applying for LPC courses but also undergraduates and those intending to take CPE. Sponsorship often requires the applicant to enter into a contract providing financial support to the student in return for a commitment to work for the firm for a specified period of time and, perhaps, including during vacations.

Sponsorship agreements do not affect your duties and responsibilities as a trainee solicitor under the Training Regulations of the Law Society and you should think carefully about the commitments which are being asked of you before you enter into an agreement.

Sponsorship information can be obtained from university/college careers offices in the CSU Publication *Legal ROGET*, (see below) or by enquiring with firms in the area in which you are hoping to work. Alternatively, contact the local Law Society to enquire whether there are any sponsoring firms in that area. Higher Education Careers Services may be approached by large firms wishing to recruit, and those belonging to the Association of Graduate Careers Advisory Services have an arrangement whereby you may be able to seek help from your AGCAS adviser in the careers service of your local university or college of higher education.

Law Society Loan Scheme

This scheme is run by two of the four major banks, National Westminster and Barclays. It is available to students on the CPE or the Legal Practice Course. Details of these schemes are provided by the banks involved

Application Procedure

The Law Society provides application forms for this scheme. Once the student has completed the form, it must be returned to the Law Society for authorisation.

It must be stressed that those applicants who require finance for the Legal Practice Course must be fully enrolled members of the Law Society with a valid certificate of completion of the academic stage of training and for those who require finance for CPE evidence of the applicant's certificate of eligibility must be available. Once the Law Society has authorised the loan, it is forwarded to the nominated bank, from where it is administered by the bank. The Law Society has no further contact concerning the loan.

Some useful sources of information

Grants to Students – A Brief Guide

Department for Education
Elizabeth House, York Road,
London SE1 7PH

Legal ROGET

Central Services Unit
Crawford House, Precinct Centre
Manchester M13 9EP

Information Booklet on
Career Development Loans

Freepost Career Development
PO Box 99, Sudbury, Suffolk CO10 6BR

Addresses

For Local Education Authority Addresses

The Education Authorities Directory and Annual, The School Government Publishing Company Limited, Darby House, Bletchingley Road, Merstham, Redhill RH1 3DN

(or your local telephone directory)

The Law Society

General Information   General Enquiries Department,
                                       113 Chancery Lane, London, WC2 1PL

CPE and LSF Enquiries   The Legal Education Department,
                                       Professional Standards and Development
                                       Directorate, Ipsley Court, Redditch,
                                       Worcestershire B98 0TD.
                                       Tel 071 242 1222 or for local calls
                                       0527 517141

4   A CAREER AS A BARRISTER

Although changes are now taking place within the legal profession, barristers have traditionally been regarded as 'specialists' who work through solicitors in the same way that medical consultants work through general practitioners. In this way the solicitor consults barristers on aspects of the law in the case of complex legal issues and the latter will appear in court on behalf of solicitors' clients.

Such cases will initially be prepared by the solicitor, after which the barrister will be required to undertake a considerable amount of detailed research before presenting his client's case in court. The knowledge required in some specialisations is quite considerable and those barristers specialising in patent work often have science or engineering degrees.

Most barristers will specialise, the main alternatives being in common law (family law, crime, divorce, etc) or chancery (company law, tax, property, trust or estates work). In either case barristers usually specialise in one of these branches, particularly in London.

All barristers, however, do not necessarily spend most of their time in court. Much depends on the type of specialisation they follow. Common law barristers will undoubtedly be involved in court work; those working in chancery, however, will not.

The Bar is a relatively small profession with approximately 6,000 in practice, at least 75 per cent of them in London. Barristers share chambers and the services of barristers' clerks and since they are not permitted to set up in practice on their own on completion of their pupillage, they are required to find a 'seat' in chambers. Once in chambers, however, they are in effect 'self-employed' and are dependent on solicitors offering them work, through their clerks in chambers.

After 15 years of experience at the Bar, a barrister can apply to the Lord Chancellor for a patent as a Queen's Counsel (taking silk). It is necessary to take silk in order to become a high court judge.

Barristers' Clerks should also be mentioned here since they occupy an important place in the lives of any barrister. A senior clerk and the juniors working with him service all the barristers in one set of chambers. They act as an intermediary between solicitors and barristers, decide which cases their barristers will accept and decide which barrister in their chambers will deal with a case and fix the fee. They will also arrange the times when the case will be heard and subsequently receive a percentage of each barrister's fees. In consequence their income can be very high (sometimes more than the barrister). Recruitment is open to school leavers with a good educational background. Competition is considerable and training is mainly 'on the job'.

Skills

The following skills have been identified as relevant to barristers and will be taught to students as part of the vocational course: Legal Research, Fact Management, Opinion Writing, Interviewing, Negotiating, Drafting and Advocacy.

Initially, in order to prepare students for the discrete areas of skills training, there will be short courses in Communication Skills, Writing Skills for the Barrister and Numeracy.

Students will learn these skills mainly by gaining experience of them in dealing with realistic sets of case papers. A central part of the learning process will be role play and students will be encouraged to make full use of the equipment for videoing performances in their roles. Students will be called upon to interview one another, role playing both lay and professional clients; to negotiate solutions to legal problems with one another, to draft documents and pleadings as required; to role play the conduct of cases in courts and tribunals both as barristers and as others in the trial process; to carry out legal research using original source materials and practitioners' works; to write opinions on the merits of a case and on the evidence, and to experience how to develop and present a theory of the case and find a solution to the problem presented.

Have You the Right Qualities to be a Barrister?

a) Would you enjoy doing very detailed research into a subject?
b) Would you enjoy unravelling the legal intricacies of a subject?
c) Would you enjoy being able to learn about and then speak knowledgeably on the most technical aspects of a subject and even examine an expert witness?
d) Could you stand up in front of your class and explain a very obscure subject so that the rest of the class could understand it?

Qualifying to be a Barrister

The process of training to become a practising barrister in England and Wales is divided into three stages which must be completed in the following order.

The Academic Stage

This stage is completed by studying Law or a combination of Law and another subject at degree level, or alternatively it is possible to study any subject to degree level which is then followed by a special one-year Common Professional Examination (CPE) course. The third route is to be accepted by an Inn of Court as a non-graduate mature student and then follow a two-year CPE course at the University of the West of England (formerly Bristol University), Manchester Metropolitan University, Northumbria University or Westminster University.

There are four Inns of Court – Lincoln's Inn, Inner Temple, Middle Temple or Gray's Inn – all in London. Prospective entrants to the Bar must be admitted as student members of one of the Inns of Court – the minimum entry requirement being a first degree with at least second-class honours. To practise as a barrister students must complete both the academic and vocational stages of training, keep eight dining terms at their Inn of Court, take the full-time vocational courses at the Inns of Court School of Law, be called to the Bar and serve one year's pupillage.

The Vocational Stage

The method of completing this stage of training varies according to whether a student does or does not intend to practise as a Member of the Bar of England and Wales or the Channel Islands, or in the territory of any Member State of the European Community.

A student who does not intend to practise in England and Wales is required to complete the Vocational Stage by examination by entering and passing the Bar examination set for that purpose.

The Vocational Course aims to provide a practical training in the specialist skills required by barristers, and to ensure competence in those skills. This will be achieved through practice in the tasks most commonly performed by junior members of the Bar during the early years of practice and most particularly, in the second six months of pupillage. Approximately two-thirds of class contact time in the course will be devoted to skills training, whilst no more than 40 per cent of all class contact time will be spent acquiring new knowledge. All aspects of the course will emphasise the need for a professional approach to work, and will encourage the students to develop a respect for the principles of professional conduct. The student's successful completion of the course will be assessed in the practical work, and in tests and examinations carried out during the year.

Courses in preparation for the Bar Examination are at present offered by various colleges including:

Holborn College
200 Greyhound Road
London W14 9RY

London Guildhall University
Faculty of Law
84 Moorgate
London EC2M 6SQ

Thames Valley University
School of Law and Social Science
St Mary's Road
Ealing
London W5 5RF

Manchester Metropolitan University
Department of Law
John Dalton Building
Chester Street
Manchester M1 5GD

South Bank University
Department of Law and Government
Faculty of Management and Policy Studies
103 Borough Road,
London SE1 0AA

Westminster University
Faculty of Law
Red Lion Square
London WC1R 4SR

Students should note that all institutions offering courses in preparation for the Bar Examination are independent of the CLE, and have sole control over admissions to their courses and the discipline of students attending them. Students should apply direct to the institutions for information on course dates, fees and registration procedures.

Pupillage

This is a twelve-month period of apprenticeship which is, in general, served with one or more practising barristers.

On successful completion of this third stage of training a barrister is qualified to enter practice.

Full details of training as a barrister are available from the Council of Legal Education, 4 Gray's Inn Place, London WC1R 5DX.

5   CHOOSING A DEGREE COURSE

Law Degree Courses

If you decide to choose a law degree course it is useful to start by understanding what qualities are sought by admissions tutors. Here are some quotations:

'We look for qualities of perseverance, a logical mind able to exclude the irrelevant, patience, and, ideally, common sense.'

'Law as a degree should really be regarded as a liberal education, rather than a vocational subject.'

'The primary criterion applied in selecting applicants for interview is evidence of general ability. Clear-mindedness, a conceptual approach and a high level of oral facility are also advantageous.'

'Four qualities are highly desirable, exactness, conciseness, strict relevance and system. The best school subjects to take are those which encourage these qualities; the worst are those which ensure success not by the exercise of the grey matter, but by wordy expositions of memorised facts of a merely descriptive nature. A widespread notion which has to be scotched is that science is a worse preparation than arts subjects for law.'

The following is taken from the Bristol University prospectus.

What Qualities of Mind do you Need?

The academic study of law involves the acquisition of the basic knowledge of a subject, the understanding of it, the ability to apply such knowledge relevantly and accurately, and a willingness to criticise the existing law intelligently. Students must be prepared to think for themselves and to develop their own ideas.

It follows that successful law students will have the ability to:

a)   understand and assimilate many concepts, principles, rules and large amounts of detailed information;

b)   apply their knowledge in a logical, accurate, intelligent manner;

c)   analyse subtle legal distinctions; and

d)   develop their critical faculties so that they can approach the study of law from a reforming, constructive viewpoint. The student who has assimilated the necessary materials and has learnt to think accurately about legal concepts will have the necessary tools to speculate on what the law ought to be – an important part of legal study.

A Popular Misconception

Despite all the attention given to Criminal Law in the newspapers and on television, a brief glance at the Bristol prospectus will reveal how misconceived it would be to equate the study of Law with an analysis of the Criminal Law. In fact, in the Bristol Law Faculty, Criminal Law is only one of the 14 courses which students undertake for the LLB degree. This is not to say that the study of Criminal Law is unimportant: rather, it is to emphasise that any law course involves a study of various categories of law. One important area of law relates to the obligations that citizens owe each other (studied, for example, in Tort and Contract); another body of law is concerned with rights over property (for example, Land Law); a third is the relationship between the citizen and state institutions (for example, Administrative Law). Students may expect to undertake courses in each of these areas.

The following books should prove useful to anyone who wishes to obtain a general idea of what the study of law may involve:

P Kenny, *Studying Law*.
J A G Griffith, *The Politics of the Judiciary*
P S Atiyah, *Law and Modern Society*.
P Harris, *An Introduction to Law*.
P D Fraser, *How to Pass Law Exams*.

Non-Law Degree Courses

Choosing a degree course will depend on several factors, and one of these must be the motivation and interest to be able to pursue a subject for the next three years.

Some students are ready to make career decisions at 17 or 18 and choose degree courses leading to specific career areas such as law, business studies, surveying, architecture, etc. Others, however, are not sure, and they may turn to their 'A' Level subjects as a basis for future studies.

Whatever the degree subject, the level of degree course to be followed initially is that of the Bachelor or first degree which is offered by universities and colleges of higher education (not to be confused with colleges of further education, which offer courses for boys and girls at 16, as an alternative to staying on at school), institutes of higher education and specialist colleges, eg colleges of agriculture, art, etc. The exception to this rule concerns some Scottish universities in which the first degree is a Master of Arts degree (MA) awarded to students in the Scottish system who usually start their courses one year earlier than students at English and Welsh universities. These MA courses normally last four years. An MA in Scotland is equivalent to a BA in English and Welsh universities. The most well known Bachelor degrees are BA and BSc (Bachelor of Arts and Sciences). There are others, however, such as the LLB (Bachelor of Laws), MB (Bachelor of Medicine), BEng (Engineering), BEd (Education), BMus (Music), BTech (Technology). All these degrees are equivalent to each other.

Honours degrees are divided into 'classes' – 1st, 2nd (sub-divided into 2:1 and 2:2) and 3rd. Ordinary and Pass degrees are awarded to those who fail some exams on the 'Honours' course.

Types of Degree Course

There are six types of courses:

a)   *Single Honours courses* This is a study of one subject, although at some universities and colleges it may be possible to study other subsidiary subjects for part of the course.

b)   *Joint Honours courses* These courses involve the study of two subjects. These subjects might have similarities, eg Mathematics and Computer Science, or French and Italian, or they might be quite different, eg Geography and Music. It is worth noting that there may be fewer places on these courses and higher standards of entry may be required.

c)   *Combined Honours courses* These courses usually involve the study of several subjects, eg the Combined courses at Leicester and Newcastle Universities and the General Honours course at Birmingham University.

d)   *Sandwich courses* These courses consist of periods of work experience which are combined with theoretical study at university or college. Experience with firms and other organisations can be a great asset to the student who may often be offered a job with the firm at the end of his or her degree course. (Sandwich courses in Law are offered by Brunel University and Bristol (UWE), Bournemouth University, Nottingham Trent University and Sheffield Hallam University.) The thick sandwich course usually concerns those sixth formers who have managed to obtain a sponsorship. On leaving school, students usually spend a year with their firm on full pay. This is followed by three years at university, returning to the firm in the fifth year.

e)   *External Degree courses* 'External' degrees are awarded on satisfactory completion of the prescribed examinations by the University of London to students who have prepared themselves for the examinations on full-time or part-time courses at colleges outside the University of London's Federation of Colleges or by distance learning courses or independent private study. These degrees have exactly the same standing as degrees obtained by full-time study at universities and colleges of higher education. A number of colleges offer courses leading to University of London external degrees and Holborn College, one of the largest independent colleges of law in the United Kingdom and an Associate College of Wolverhampton University, offers courses leading to the University of London external LLB (Honours) degree in Law and BSc (Economics) degrees in Accountancy, Management Studies or Economics and Management Studies.

f)   *Franchised Degree Courses* As higher education evolves in the 1990s flexibility is the key to many of the new courses. Many institutions are franchising their courses at various levels to other institutions in the United Kingdom and overseas.

In October 1990 Holborn College in London was validated by the CNAA to take a franchise of the LLB (Honours) Degree from Wolverhampton University and is now an Associate College of the University. This degree programme provides one of the widest selections of course options for an LLB (Honours) Degree available in the United Kingdom. Application has been made to the Department for Education for award status for United Kingdom 'home students' at Holborn College and if this is granted it will amount to approximately £695 fees payment in addition to maintenance grants where applicable.

Holborn College also offers an LLB (Honours) Degree by distance learning with optional support tuition in conjunction with Wolverhampton University which gives students total flexibility in the way in which they prepare for a law degree. Students may transfer between full-time, part-time and distance learning modes as personal circumstances change through the period of study.

Choosing a degree course other than Law could stem from considering 'A' Level subject options. In the first instance you could choose your favourite 'A' Level subject or subjects (at least you have a good idea of what they involve). Talk to your tutors about a possible degree course in these subjects and read through prospectuses to obtain a better idea of the topics to be covered.

However, it is not just necessary to choose the 'A' Level subject you enjoy the most. Each 'A' Level subject is part of a larger family of similar subjects, and with your interest in other 'A' Level subjects there could be several obvious connections which will produce alternative ideas.

Let us take a look at some 'A' Level subjects and appropriate degree courses which would enable you to go on to train as a solicitor or barrister after graduation.

Arts and Humanities Subjects

Ancient History – Archaeology, Biblical Studies, Greek, Latin, Classical Studies, Religious Studies and Philosophy.

British Government and Politics – Economics, European Studies, History, Law, Public Administration, Strategic Studies.

Economics – Accountancy (Actuarial work), Banking, Business and Business Finance, Estate Management, Operational Research, Planning, Quantity Surveying, Social Studies.

English – Anglo-Saxon, Drama, European Literature, Journalism, Languages, Librarianship.

Geography – African, Asian and European Studies, Earth Sciences and Geology, Environmental Studies, Estate Management, Fisheries Management, Land Economy, Meteorology, Oceanography, Town and Country Planning.

History – American Studies, Anthropology, Biblical Studies, Law, History (covering various countries and continents of the world).

Languages – Apart from those languages being studied to 'A' Level it is also possible to start new languages from scratch on many university courses, eg Arabic, Chinese, Japanese, Scandinavian, East European, Near Eastern and Far Eastern languages.

Religious Studies – Archaeology, Education, History, Philosophy, Psychology, Social Administration.

Science Subjects

Biology – Agricultural and Animal Sciences, Biological Sciences, Dentistry, Dietetics, Ecology, Environmental Science, Forestry, Horticulture, Marine Biology, Medicine, Nursing, Nutrition, Occupational Therapy, Pharmacology, Pharmacy, Psychology, Speech Science, Veterinary Science, Zoology.

Chemistry – As above and also Biochemistry, Chemical Engineering, Colour Chemistry, Food Science, Fuel Science, Oil Technology, Textile Chemistry.

Geology – Geography, Mining and Mineral Exploitation, Mining Surveying.

Mathematics – Accountancy, Actuarial Science, Business Studies, Computer Science, Economics, Engineering, Operational Research.

Physics – Building and Building Services Engineering (Heating – Refrigeration – Acoustics), all engineering subjects, Materials Science, Naval Architecture.

Other Subjects

Having read through these lists you may form ideas about some course options but *beware*. Do not reject courses you have never heard of and do not assume you know very much about those courses you think are familiar! The following list will give you just a taste of what might be involved when choosing some subjects to study.

Agriculture – The choice may lie between the very practical type of farming courses or those which have a greater emphasis on agricultural science.

American Studies – This covers the history and literature of the USA (and including Canada at Birmingham University).

Archaeology – This usually involves a study of archaeology in the British Isles and the Mediterranean countries. These courses sometimes include Ancient History.

Art – Practical work courses are offered at some universities as well as at the colleges. The History of Art, Architecture or Design may also be studied; in some cases both practical and theoretical work is done on the same course.

Biology/Biochemistry – Choices include a bias towards Medicine, Nutrition, Agriculture, Pharmacology, Biotechnology, Marine, Plant, Fishery and Animal Sciences.

Business Studies – This is a very wide field (see *The Way In – Business and Management* (HLT Publications)) and covers accountancy and financial management, management services, marketing, sales, personnel work, retail management, textile management, estate management, and hotel management. In some universities, business can be combined with a language, at Birmingham, Kingston, Leeds,

Loughborough, Manchester Metropolitan, Sheffield Hallam and Nottingham Trent. European Business Studies is an option in several universities, eg Central Lancashire, Humberside, Middlesex, Nottingham Trent and at Buckinghamshire College. London University's external degree in Management Studies or Economics and Management Studies (both BSc Econ) can be studied on a three-year full-term programme at Holborn College. (Offers for all these courses are in the DD–EE range.) It is also possible to take a one-year London University Diploma in Economics at Holborn College and to transfer to the degree course at the end of the year.

Chemistry – Courses can be taken with one other subject in Year 1, eg at Bristol, Liverpool, Lancaster; or with a language, at Nottingham and East Anglia; or with a year in Europe or USA, at East Anglia, Surrey; or as sandwich courses, at Bath, Aston, Loughborough, Brunel.

Drama – There is a practical performance bias at Aberystwyth, East Anglia and Hull. (Dance is offered at Surrey, Birmingham and Bretton Hall College).

Environmental Science – This subject has an emphasis on Biology/Geography, at Bradford and Sheffield Universities, or with Chemistry/Geology at Kent and Sussex, or with Physics at Lancaster, or with Geography/Planning at University College London or Sheffield (Hallam), or a study of Environmental Health at Salford, Leeds Metropolitan, and Greenwich Universities.

Engineering – Many specialisations are offered, eg Electrical/Electronics (including telecommunications and systems), Chemical (including Nuclear, Fuel and Energy), Mechanical and Production, Civil and Structural Engineering.

French – Courses could have a bias toward literature at some universities, such as Oxbridge and Durham, or alternatively as European Studies courses, at Surrey and Bath or Cardiff (European Community Studies).

History – Courses may offer a choice between British, European, Ancient, Medieval or Modern History or the History of the World, eg Newcastle (Russia and Latin America), or Warwick (Mexico and Cuba).

Materials Science – This is an ideal course for those with equal interests between Physics and Chemistry and leading to careers in metallurgy, polymers, glasses, ceramics. (There is a real shortage of graduates in this subject area.)

Mathematics – A choice is available from Pure Maths, Applied Maths, Statistics and Operational Research.

Psychology – This includes Social or Human Psychology, eg at Bradford and Loughborough, Educational, Occupational and Clinical Psychology at Bangor and Cardiff.

Religious Studies – This subject may cover the origins of Christianity, Islam, Judaism, Buddhism, but studies may also involve Biblical Studies and Theology.

Social Administration – This subject covers aspects of public administration, housing, health and mental illness and other similar topics.

Social Studies – Courses involve the nature and development of modern society (Economics, Politics, Sociology, Geography) and methods of social investigation.

6 LAW COURSES IN THE UK

First degree courses in law all follow a similar pattern and consist of both compulsory and optional subjects. Compulsory subjects cover legal principles, eg Contract, Criminal Law, Constitutional Law, Land Law, Tort and Equity. Optional subjects, however, cover a very wide field and, for example, at Newcastle University include Civil Liberties, Consumer Protection, Environmental Law, European Community Law, Insurance and Partnership, and Public International Law.

The following universities and colleges offer degree courses in Law and combinations of subjects with Law (NB Scottish institutions also offer Scottish Law).

Aberdeen, Aberystwyth, Anglia Polytechnic University, Belfast, Birmingham, Bristol, Bristol (University of the West of England), Brunel, Buckingham, Cambridge, Cardiff, Central England, Central Lancashire, De Montfort, Derby, Dundee, Durham, East Anglia, East London, Edinburgh, Essex, Exeter, Glamorgan, Greenwich, Hertfordshire, Holborn College, Huddersfield, Hull, Kent, Kingston, Lancaster, Leeds, Leeds Metropolitan, Leicester, Liverpool, Liverpool John Moores, London (King's), London (LSE), London (Queen Mary/Westfield), London (SOAS), London (University College), Luton, Manchester, Manchester Metropolitan, Middlesex, Nene College, Newcastle, North London, Northumbria, Nottingham, Nottingham Trent, Oxford, Oxford Brookes, Reading, Sheffield, Sheffield Hallam, Southampton, Southampton Institute, South Bank, Staffordshire, Sussex, Swansea, Swansea Institute, Teesside, Thames Valley, Warwick, Westminster, Wolverhampton

Law with options
Aberdeen (Economics or French or German or Spanish), Northumbria

Law and Accounting
Aberystwyth, Belfast, Brighton, East Anglia, Edinburgh, Kingston, Manchester, Newcastle, Oxford Brookes, Plymouth, Sheffield Hallam (International Financial Studies), Southampton, Southampton Institute, Staffordshire, Teesside, Thames Valley

Law and American Studies/American Legal Systems
East Anglia (American Legal Systems), Keele (American Studies), Staffordshire (American Studies), Sussex (English and American Studies, North American Studies)

Law and Anthropology
East London, Kent, London (LSE), London (SOAS), Oxford Brookes

Law and Art
Anglia Polytechnic University (Art History, Graphic Arts), East London (Fine Art, Art Design and Film History), Oxford Brookes (Fine Art, Visual Studies), Staffordshire (History of Art and Design)

Law and Asian or African Language
London (SOAS)

Law and Astrophysics
Keele

Law and Biology
Buckingham, East London

Law and Business Studies/Management Science/Administrative Studies
Aberystwyth, Anglia Polytechnic University, Birmingham, Coventry, East London, Edinburgh, Glasgow Caledonian, Humberside, Keele, Liverpool John Moores, Oxford Brookes (also Retail Management), Plymouth, Southampton Institute, Swansea

Law and Cartography
Oxford Brookes

Law and Catering Management
Oxford Brookes

Law and Celtic
Edinburgh

Law and Chemistry
Bristol, Exeter, Keele, Oxford Brookes

Law and Chinese
Leeds

Law and Classical Studies
Keele

Law and Advanced or Combined Studies
London (University College), Nene College

Law and Communication Studies
Anglia Polytechnic University, Staffordshire

Law and Computer Studies
East London (Business Information Systems), Keele, Oxford Brookes, Plymouth, Strathclyde, East London (New Technology)

Law and Criminal Justice
Liverpool John Moores

Law and Criminology
Keele, Sheffield

Law and Cultural Studies
East London, Staffordshire

Law and Design
East London

Law and Development Studies
London (SOAS), Staffordshire

Law and Economics
Anglia Polytechnic University, Aberystwyth, Durham, East London, Edinburgh, Keele, Kent, Leicester, London (SOAS), London (Queen Mary/Westfield), Oxford Brookes, Plymouth, Sussex, Ulster

Law and Education
East London, Keele, Oxford Brookes

Law and Electronics
Keele

Law and Engineering
London (Univ Coll) (Civil Engineering)

Law and English
Anglia Polytechnic University, East Anglia, Keele, Oxford Brookes

Law and Environmental Studies
East London, Oxford Brookes, Plymouth, Staffordshire

Law and a European Language
Aberystwyth, Central Lancashire, Kent

Law and European Legal Systems
East Anglia, Aberdeen, Kingston, Oxford, London (Kings)

Law and European Studies
Aberdeen, Anglia Polytechnic University, East London, Reading, Staffordshire, Sussex

Law and European Thought and Literature
Anglia Polytechnic University

Law (English) and European Law
London (Queen Mary/Westfield), Buckingham (also with languages), Essex

Law and Feminist Gender Studies
Staffordshire

Law and Food Science
Oxford Brookes

Law and French
Anglia Polytechnic University, Belfast, Birmingham, Bristol, Buckingham, Cardiff, De Montfort, East Anglia, East London, Edinburgh, Keele, Leeds, Leicester, Liverpool, Liverpool John Moores, London Guildhall, Manchester Metropolitan, Newcastle, Oxford Brookes, Sheffield, Staffordshire, Surrey, Swansea, Westminster, Wolverhampton

Law and French Law
Aberdeen, East Anglia, Essex, Kent, London (King's), London (LSE), London (University College), Manchester, Northumbria, Reading, Thames Valley

Law and Gender Studies
Hull

Law and Geography
Anglia Polytechnic University, Keele, Oxford Brookes, Plymouth, Staffordshire

Law and Geology
Oxford Brookes

Law and Geotechnics
Oxford Brookes

Law and German
Anglia Polytechnic University, Belfast, Bristol, Cardiff, De Montfort, East London, Edinburgh, Keele, Liverpool, London (Queen Mary/Westfield), Oxford Brookes, Sheffield, Staffordshire, Surrey, Swansea, Westminster

Law and German Law
Aberdeen, East Anglia, Kent, London (King's), London (LSE), London (University College), Thames Valley

Law and Government
London (LSE), Ulster

Law and History
Anglia Polytechnic University, East Anglia, East London, Edinburgh (also Economic History), Keele (also Ancient History and International History), Kent (also Economic and Social History), London (SOAS), London (University College), Oxford Brookes, Staffordshire, Sussex

Law and Health Studies
East London, Oxford Brookes

Law with Hispanic Studies
Belfast

Law and Human Resource Management
Keele

Law and Independent Study
East London

Law/Industrial Relations
Kent

Law and Information and Library Studies
Aberystwyth

Law and Information Technology
East London, Staffordshire

Law and Intelligent Systems
Oxford Brookes

Law and International Studies/Relations
Staffordshire, Coventry, Plymouth

Law and Italian
Anglia Polytechnic University, Belfast, Cardiff, East London

Law and Italian Law
Kent, London (University College)

Law and Japanese
Leeds, Cardiff

Law with Labour Studies
Plymouth

Law with Languages
Plymouth, Sussex

Law and Linguistics
East London

Law and Literature
East London, Staffordshire

Law and Mathematics
Anglia Polytechnic University, East London, Keele, Oxford Brookes

Law and Marketing
Oxford Brookes

Law and Media Studies
East London

Law and Microbiology
East London

Law and Microelectronics
Oxford Brookes

Law and Music
Anglia Polytechnic University, Keele, Oxford Brookes

Law and Pharmacology
East London

Law and Philosophy
Staffordshire, Edinburgh, Hull, Keele, Kent

Law and Physics/Physical Sciences
Oxford Brookes

Law and Physiology
East London

Law and Planning Studies
Oxford Brookes

Law and Politics
Aberystwyth, Anglia Polytechnic University, Belfast, Birmingham, Buckingham, Cardiff, Durham, Edinburgh, Hull, Keele, Kent, London (Queen Mary/Westfield), London (SOAS), Nottingham, Oxford Brookes, Plymouth, Southampton, Staffordshire

Law and Popular Culture
East London

Law and Psychology
Keele, Liverpool John Moores, Oxford Brookes, Plymouth, Staffordshire

Law and Psychosocial Studies
East London

Law and Publishing
Oxford Brookes

Law and Religious Studies
London (SOAS)

Law and Russian
Surrey, Swansea

Law and Social Policy
Anglia Polytechnic University, East London, Edinburgh, Kent, Plymouth, Staffordshire

Law and Social Studies
Keele, Sussex

Law and Society
Exeter

Law and Sociology
Anglia Polytechnic University, Cardiff, Durham, East London, Edinburgh, Hull, Keele, Kent, Oxford Brookes, Plymouth, Staffordshire, Warwick

Law and Spanish
Anglia Polytechnic University, Aberdeen, Buckingham, Cardiff, East London, Edinburgh, Sheffield, Staffordshire, Swansea, Westminster

Law and Spanish Law
Kent Thames Valley

Law and Third World Studies
East London

Law and Tourism
Oxford Brookes

Law and Transport
Plymouth

Law and Urban Studies
East London

Law and Welsh
Swansea

Law and Women's Studies
Anglia Polytechnic University, East London, Staffordshire

Business Law
Bournemouth, Brunel, City, Coventry, London Guildhall, Stirling, Thames Valley

Business Law and Business
Liverpool John Moores

Business Law and Financial Management
Liverpool John Moores

Business Law and French
Liverpool John Moores

Business Law and German
Liverpool John Moores

Business Law and Human Resource Management
Liverpool John Moores

Business Law and International Management
Liverpool John Moores

Business Law and Marketing
Liverpool John Moores

Conveyancing Law
Dundee Institute

Environmental Law
Greenwich

European Business Law
Coventry, Dundee Institute, Sussex

European Law
Bristol (University of the West of England), Strathclyde, Exeter, Nottingham, Trent, Thames Valley, Warwick

European Law and Languages
Bristol (University of West of England), Sussex

Maritime Law with Fisheries and Business Studies
Plymouth

Maritime Law with Hydrography
Plymouth

Maritime Law with Maritime Business
Plymouth

Maritime Law with Marine Technology
Plymouth

Maritime Law with Transport
Plymouth

Maritime Law with Underwater Studies
Plymouth

Legal Studies
Coventry, Glamorgan, Glasgow Caledonian, London Guildhall, Napier, Robert Gordon

Legal Studies and Accounting
Gwent College

Legal Studies and American Studies
Staffordshire

Legal Studies and Business
Farnborough College, Gwent College

Legal Studies and Communication Studies
Staffordshire

Legal Studies and Cultural Studies
Staffordshire

Legal Studies and Environmental Studies
Staffordshire

Legal Studies and Feminist and Gender Studies
Staffordshire

Legal Studies and French
Staffordshire, Swansea

Legal Studies and Geography
Staffordshire

Legal Studies and German
Staffordshire, Swansea

Legal Studies and History
Staffordshire

Legal Studies and History of Art
Staffordshire

Legal Studies and Information Systems
Staffordshire

Legal Studies and International Policy
Staffordshire

Legal Studies and International Relations
Staffordshire

Legal Studies with Italian
Swansea

Legal Studies and Literature
Staffordshire

Legal Studies and Philosophy
Staffordshire

Legal Studies and Policy Studies
Staffordshire

Legal Studies and Political Economy
Staffordshire

Legal Studies and Politics
Staffordshire

Legal Studies and Public Administration
Luton

Legal Studies and Psychology
Staffordshire

Legal Studies with Russian
Swansea

Legal Studies and Sociology
Staffordshire

Legal Studies and Spanish
Staffordshire, Swansea

Legal Studies with Welsh
Swansea

Legal Studies with Women's Studies
Staffordshire

European Legal Studies
Aberdeen, Kent, Lancaster, London (Kings)

Criminal Justice
Coventry, Glamorgan, Thames Valley

Criminal Justice and French
Liverpool John Moores

Criminal Justice and German
Liverpool John Moores

Criminal Justice and Policing
Central England

Criminal Justice and Politics
Liverpool John Moores

Criminal Justice and Psychology
Liverpool John Moores

Criminal Justice and Sociology
Liverpool John Moores

Criminal Justice and Women's Studies
Liverpool John Moores

Criminology and American Studies
Keele

Criminology and Ancient History
Keele

Criminology and Computer Science
Keele

Criminology and Classical Studies
Keele

Criminology and Economics
Keele

Criminology and Educational Studies
Keele

Criminology and French
Keele

Criminology and History
Keele

Criminology and Music
Keele

Criminology and Philosophy
Keele

Criminology and Psychology
Keele

Criminology and Sociology
Keele

Scots Law
Glasgow, Strathclyde

Scots Law and French
Glasgow

Scots Law and French Legal Studies
Glasgow

Scots Law and German
Glasgow

Scots Law and German Legal Studies
Glasgow

Scots Law and Spanish
Glasgow

Scots Law and Spanish Legal Studies
Glasgow

Jurisprudence and International Relations
Aberdeen

Jurisprudence and Politics
Aberdeen

Jurisprudence and Social Research
Aberdeen

Jurisprudence and Philosophy
Aberdeen

Jurisprudence and Sociology
Aberdeen

7 NEW DEVELOPMENTS IN HIGHER EDUCATION

In recent years many new developments have taken place in higher education. Traditional 'internal' and 'external' degrees continue to offer routes to first degree levels, in addition to which many colleges and universities are coming together to offer a range of degree courses.

Holborn College (the largest independent Law School in the UK), an Associate College of the University of Wolverhampton, offers the University's LLB on an internal basis, and provides one of the widest selections of course options for an LLB (Honours) Degree available in the UK.

By combining their strengths and expertise Holborn College and the School of Legal Studies at Wolverhampton have created one of the largest teaching resources in terms of staff, student numbers and the range of courses offered within the UK and Commonwealth.

The LLB (Honours) Degree is a three-year full-time programme comprising four subjects for each year. Examinations take place in May/June. The first year of the course leads to the Certificate of Higher Education in Law (Cert HE Law). The second year leads to the Diploma of Higher Education in Law (Dip HE Law) and the final year leads to the LLB Degree with or without honours. Part-time and distance learning programmes are also offered. Examination is by means of continuous assessment and unseen written examination and is the same whichever mode of study is chosen.

For this course UK and European Community students are entitled to mandatory contributions towards tuition fees and maintenance awards as appropriate from their local Education Authority.

Holborn College also offers courses for the University of London's LLB (External) degree. External degrees were first introduced by the University of London in the nineteenth century and were created for students unable to attend a full-time course at a college or 'school' of the University of London for financial or other reasons or because they did not have the necessary entry grades for admission to internal degree programmes.

Lord Flowers (a former Vice Chancellor of London University) describes external degrees in greater detail:

'The University does not have separate internal and external degrees. It has a single degree which is studied by internal and external students. The University has always refused to separate the awards available to external students from those for internal students. The reason for this policy is to ensure that the standard of achievement of internal and external students is judged on exactly the same basis. Thus the method of study is not an issue; the important test is the examination. In many instances internal and external students sit exactly the same examination papers for their degree. Where this is not the case the same examiners will have set the papers for external as for internal students. All examination papers, whether for internal or external students, are marked by University of London academic staff to exactly the same standard, and the same degree classification is used for both kinds of student.'

Both internal and external students must register as students of the University of London. On successful completion of their course all students may attend the University of London graduation ceremony where the degrees are presented by the Chancellor, HRH The Princess Royal. No distinction is made between external and internal students when the degrees are awarded.

It is a well accepted fact that 'A' Level results are not necessarily indicators of potential degree performance. Students can obtain poor 'A' Level grades for a variety of reasons – they may choose the wrong subjects, they may have poor teachers, or they may experience personal problems during their period of study. This does not mean that they are incapable of degree level study. Regrettably, because the educational system in the UK decides a student's fate on the strength of 'A' Level results, many able students are denied the opportunity of proving that they are capable of taking a degree and that their disappointing 'A' Level grades are not a true reflection of their ability. This is overcome by the lower level of offers made by Holborn College for all applicants. The offers set by the London University for LLB (External) degree students are two 'A' Level passes at Grade E. Holborn College will also consider applicants with these grades for entry to the University of Wolverhampton LLB (Honours) Degree programme. It should be noted that mature students (over 21) without formal academic qualifications are also given special consideration for admission to law courses at universities and colleges, on the basis of their post-school career development and evidence of their motivation and commitment to studying for a degree.

Holborn College students achieve high success rates in the examinations each year, largely due to the unique and carefully structured teaching system offered by the College. In addition several students obtain university convocation prizes.

In addition to the full-time law courses, facilities also exist for students to follow part-time or distance learning courses while continuing in their full-time employment. Course programmes allow flexibility in modes of study and enable students to change from distance learning study to full-time or part-time study at any stage of the course programme.

LLB degrees are recognised by the Council of Legal Education and the Law Society for entry to the vocational stage of training. Many Bar Associations world-wide also recognise the degree for entry to their Bar examinations.

Applications for courses at Holborn College are made direct or (for 1995 entry) through UCAS for the full-time University of Wolverhampton LLB degree. So students aiming for the University of London LLB (External) degree or for the Holborn College/Wolverhampton University LLB degree course programmes should submit an early application to: The Registrar, Holborn College, 200 Greyhound Road, London W14 9RY (Tel 071 385 3377). Details of the Univeristy of London's external degree can be obtained from The University of London External Programme, Room 201, Senate House, University of London, Malet Street, London WC1E 7HU. (Tel 071 636 8000).

8 APPLYING FOR DEGREE COURSES

It is often assumed that all students automatically apply only for university places. This is not so. Everyone is different, not only in their attitudes towards higher education but also in the subjects they wish to study, where they wish to study and what their ultimate career targets may be.

You must therefore consider all aspects of your application including your objectives and in particular your abilities.

Your success or failure in obtaining a place will be largely determined by your exam results and also by your projected grades at 'A' Level, BTEC and GNVQ examinations as shown on your referees' report.

This is why a careful strategy is needed. *Never assume you will get the place you want at the university or college you prefer.* YOU MUST CONSIDER ALL THE ALTERNATIVES.

How can you do this?

a) Choose your course and check the prospectuses of each university and college offering the course.

b) Having decided which institutions offer interesting courses then refer to *The Complete Degree Course Offers* (Trotman & Co £14.95). This is the only reference book which lists the courses offered in all universities and colleges and provides information on the selection policies adopted, including the level of offers made to applicants, interview questions, completion of the UCAS form and many other aspects which concern your chances of an acceptance.

Obtain advice from your 'A' Level subject tutors concerning the grades you could achieve in the examinations. In this way you can judge your chances of being considered by the university or college of your initial choice. If your chances do not look too hopeful, consider those other institutions which might seriously consider you.

Universities are generally more popular than other institutions and because of this their offers are usually the highest. The basis of any application strategy, however, is to cover yourself in case your 'A' Level grades do not match the offers made by your universities. All universities set their grades against the number of applications and the number of places available; thus the more popular the institution the higher the offer.

The most popular institutions, however, must never be regarded necessarily as the 'best'. In the case of law courses, most institutions are offering the same type of course and only the optional subjects are likely to differ between one institution and the next. The most popular institutions are usually those located in popular geographical areas such as Oxford, Cambridge, Bristol, Durham, Exeter, Warwick and Nottingham which attracts many students because of its campus.

YOUR STRATEGY must be to make sure that you include on your application forms some institutions which may make you lower offers. In this way you will cover yourself against a poor exam result.

In addition to exam results, however, some admissions tutors place quite a lot of importance on interviews. Interviews come in all 'shapes and sizes'. Sometimes it will be a straightforward 'one to one' interview. In other cases you may face two, three or even (rarely) four interviewers.

In the case of law interviews, however, admissions tutors will expect you to be 'well read': to be familiar with current legal issues and in prominent law cases which have aroused much public discussion.

(*The Complete Degree Course Offers* gives advice on how to complete the UCAS forms and also lists the questions which have been asked in past years and whilst interviews will vary from year to year you will be able to judge what admissions tutors expect you to know.)

Addresses of universities and colleges appear in Chapter 12.

Application

Details of the application procedures are set out in the *UCAS Handbook* which is available with the UCAS application form from UCAS, Fulton House, Jessop Avenue, Cheltenham, Glos GL50 3SH.

For those aiming for careers in law there are two main alternatives: (a) for universities and some colleges, applications are submitted through the UCAS scheme on one application form; (b) for other colleges, which are not in the UCAS scheme (eg Holborn College), applications are made direct to the college concerned.

Once you have decided on the course of study you wish to follow you *must check* the subjects required by the university or college and also by the Faculty or Department of the university.

There are two types of entry requirements: general requirements and course requirements.

General Requirements

Each institution stipulates certain GCSE (or equivalent) subject requirements *for all their courses*, irrespective of whether or not these are arts, science or social science courses. ('AS' Level, 'AO' Level or 'A' Level passes are also acceptable instead of GCSE Grades A–C or 'O' Level passes.)

(Check with university prospectuses that you have the right general requirements for your chosen course at the institution to which you intend to apply).

'A' Levels, 'AS' Levels, GCSE (or equivalent)

Minimum entry requirements by way of the numbers of 'A' Levels, 'AS' Levels and GCSE subjects are also stipulated by each university. In the majority of cases most

42

students will automatically qualify because of the subjects being taken in these examinations. It is, however, wise to check these requirements, particularly if you only achieved Grade A–C passes in a small number of subjects at GCSE or equivalent. For example, the minimum entry requirement at all universities is that of two 'A' Level passes and three Grade A–C passes in the GCSE exams. THESE PASSES MUST BE IN DIFFERENT SUBJECTS.

Course Requirements

Many different subjects are offered at 'A' Level – including several subjects of a vocational nature such as Accountancy, Art, Business Studies, Theatre Studies, Communication Studies and Psychology, Music, Home Economics, Engineering Drawing and Technology.

Many university courses have a very strong academic (non-vocational) bias, the purpose of the course being to provide you with a broad 'education' and not a 'training' for a specific job, and consequently universities often tend to prefer the purely academic subjects such as English, Geography, History, Religious Studies, Languages and Science subjects. For certain courses, therefore, they may not accept the more vocational 'A' Level subjects, eg Art, Engineering, Drawing, etc. CHECK THE LIST OF APPROVED SUBJECTS IN THE PROSPECTUS.

It must also be noted that some 'A' Level subjects are similar in subject matter, such as Art and the History of Art, and Law and Constitutional Law, and these subjects may only be counted as one 'A' Level, even though you may have chosen them as two separate subjects for exam purposes.

Now let us take a look at the application scheme in more detail.

For entry to higher education in the United Kingdom at the present time, there are two main application routes into degree courses. These routes cover applications for:

- Courses in universities and colleges and institutes of higher education, in their affiliated colleges and institutions of higher education – through UCAS (the Universities and Colleges Admissions Service).

- Art and design courses in some universities and colleges of higher education – through ADAR (Art and Design Admissions Registry).

UCAS APPLICATIONS TO UNIVERSITY AND COLLEGE COURSES

The Universities and Colleges Admissions Service (UCAS) deals with applications for admission to all full-time and sandwich first degree, Diploma of Higher Education and Higher National Diploma courses in all United Kingdom universities (except the Open University) and colleges and institutions of higher education.

The UCAS procedures are designed to give applicants freedom to make responsible choices of course and institution, while giving universities and colleges freedom to select their own students, using whatever criteria and selection methods they favour.

UCAS does not recruit on behalf of universities and colleges, nor does it advise applicants on their choice of courses. Academic considerations are the concern of applicants, in conjunction with their careers teachers, parents, other advisers and the universities and colleges themselves.

Entry requirements

Before applying to universities and colleges, applicants should check that by the time they plan to start their course they will have the required qualifications. Details of entry requirements are available direct from the universities and colleges.

Applicants will need to fulfil:

(i)   the *general* entry requirements for degree or DipHE or HND courses

(ii)   any *specific* requirements to enter a particular course; for instance study of a specified subject at 'A' or 'AS' Level, GCSE, BTEC or GNVQ qualifications. The course requirements are set out in prospectuses.

All potential applicants should ask the advice of teachers or university and college advisers before submitting their application.

The application process

Details of the application procedures are set out in the UCAS *Handbook* which is available with the UCAS application form and acknowledgement card from schools, colleges and careers offices during the summer before the year of entry. Other applicants can obtain the *Handbook*, form and card direct from UCAS, PO Box 67, Cheltenham, Glos GL50 3SF, sending a self-addressed label with their request.

Applications for places should be submitted between 1 September and 15 December (or between 1 September and 15 October if you are including Oxford or Cambridge in your university choices) in the year before taking 'A'/'AS' Levels. You should send in your UCAS form as soon as possible after 1 September. Although UCAS forwards applications received after 16 December to the universities or colleges concerned, institutions' admissions tutors will only consider them at their discretion.

The normal procedure is as follows:

1   You should complete your UCAS application form in black ink and hand it with your fee to your educational referee.

2   The referee completes the confidential report and sends your form and fee to UCAS which then records your details.

3   UCAS acknowledges receipt of your form and sends you a personal application number.

4   UCAS sends reduced-size copies of your form to the universities/colleges you have named on the form.

5   Each university/college considers your application and subsequently informs UCAS of its decision. (Applicants may hear unofficially from the institutions).

6   UCAS notifies applicants of the institutions' decisions.

7   You reply through UCAS to any offers made by the universities/colleges.

You do not have to reply to any university/college offers until you have received your last decision. If you know before then that you definitely want to accept firmly one of the offers, you can do so. However, it is not advisable to accept firmly an offer until you are *absolutely* sure that this is the university/college you want to commit yourself to attending.

You may decline any offer you receive before you have received all your decisions in the UCAS scheme. However, you cannot change your mind later and accept that offer.

If you have received more than one university/college offer, UCAS will send you – with your last decision – a statement of all your decisions in the scheme, a reply slip and an explanatory leaflet.

You will be asked to reply to your offers within 14 days of receiving the statement of decisions, but there will be a dispensation for you to delay replying to your offers if you have yet to attend an open day or group visit at one or more of the universities/colleges concerned. You will not lose the offers made to you provided that your replies are received by UCAS by 15 May, but you should reply quickly after your visit(s).

If you have accepted firmly a conditional offer (CF) you can also hold one additional offer (either conditional or unconditional) as an insurance (CI or UI). Normally the insurance offer would be one which specifies lower grades. A typical 'A' Level applicant's record might read as follows:

Conditional offer - Firmly accepted (CF) - Grades BBC
Conditional offer - Insurance (CI) - Grades BCC

If your results are not as good as you had hoped and you cannot meet the offer of the university/college you have firmly accepted but can fulfil the conditions of the insurance offer, you are committed to going to the insurance institution for the specified course.

If you do not inform UCAS of your acceptance of a firm offer and (if appropriate) an insurance offer, it will not be possible to hold the offers open and they will be declined by UCAS on your behalf.

If you leave any boxes blank on the statement of decisions reply slip, UCAS will treat the offers concerned as declined and you will lose them. For example, if you have entered your firm acceptance but have not entered an insurance, UCAS will decline all your other offers, and you will lose the opportunity to hold an insurance offer.

Once you have replied to your offers, UCAS will send you a final statement of your replies and all the decisions made.

UCAS does not make decisions: it sends to you the decisions of the universities/colleges to which you have replied. It cannot change an institution's decision. If you need advice or more information, write direct to the institution.

8   The UCAS Clearing scheme operates from late August and throughout September. Its purpose is to try to match applicants without an offer with suitable courses where there are vacancies. Vacancy information is available via a number of network systems and national newspapers. Details of these services and any other sources of vacancy information are given in a leaflet sent to all applicants when they become eligible for Clearing.

UCAS Timetable

1 September..........................UCAS begins accepting applications.

15 October............................Deadline for applications (including Oxford or Cambridge) to reach UCAS.

15 December   ....Deadline for all other applications to reach UCAS.

16 December – 14 August ......Late applications distributed by UCAS to up to eight choices of university/college, but institutions will consider these at their discretion.

Late July/Early September......Confirmation of offers. UCAS tells you whether or not universities/colleges have confirmed conditional offers. If you are unsuccessful or received no offers earlier in the year, you will be sent Clearing instructions automatically.

Throughout September...........Remaining university/college places filled through Clearing.

PLEASE NOTE:

•   You are not required to reply to any university/college offers until you have received your last decision.

•   Do not send a firm acceptance to more than one offer.

•   Do not try to alter a firm acceptance.

•   Send a withdrawal slip to UCAS at once if you decide not to go to university/ college this year.

•   Remember to tell the institutions and UCAS if you either change your address, or change your examination board, subjects or arrangements.

When completing the UCAS forms special attention must be given to Section 10 since it is the only section on the form in which you can 'speak for yourself'. It is in this section that your character and interests can emerge and if you are applying for a vocational course such as Medicine or Law then you should be able to provide information about your interests in these fields, such as hospital employment or visits to the law courts etc.

For vocational courses, motivation is extremely important and inevitably applicants will wish to impress the admissions tutor. This, however, should not be done by stating how clever, imaginative, hard-working or deserving you are (it has been known for applicants to write glowing references for themselves in this section!). Your teachers will submit their references concerning your attitude and your ability in the examinations (including their assessment of what grades you will probably achieve at 'A' Level).

If you are applying for a vocational course, such as business studies, then work experience is extremely important.

A simple statement, for example, that you have worked on the cashout at a supermarket is not enough. Try to describe what you learned whilst doing it. Customer problems and attitudes. How did you deal with difficult customers? Did difficult customers fall into any particular age range? What problems did they cause? How did you get on with your fellow workers? Was there a good spirit among the workforce? What did other assistants feel about the management? Was the store well managed? If not, what were the problems? What problems did the management face? Could these problems be easily overcome or were they dictated by Head Office? Was the store well laid out? Was it necessary to make changes to the store layout to increase sales? Was it a profitable store? If not, why not. What was the customer profile – were the majority of shoppers teenagers, middle-age female or old people?

By describing some of these aspects of your work experience in detail you will have proved that you are aware of what business is about, that you are alert and, above all, that you have taken a real interest in at least one aspect of business. This also applies to other types of work experience.

Some people find it difficult to fill these sections, but others run out of space very quickly! Firstly, you do not have to write an essay. You can save space by not writing in prose. You need to plan it out carefully beforehand, however, and get your parents to help you – they will probably be able to remember some of the things you have done in the past years which you have forgotten all about. This is indeed the purpose of this section. Admissions tutors want a 'profile' of the type of person you are – your interests and your achievements.

It is usual to go back in time about three years – the fact that you were a milk monitor eight years ago in primary school will probably not carry much weight. However, if you won a national speaking competition or achieved something equally notable at an early age then this might be worth mentioning.

Plan out the section methodically. This could be done in sub-sections as follows.

School activities

Positions of responsibility, eg school prefect, chairperson, treasurer, secretary of any committees, sporting activities (indoor and outdoor sports), team membership with dates (this will show how long you have been involved with the team). Field courses (more than one day) attended as part of your studies. Business games, school visits abroad. Musical activities – school orchestra – instruments played (if you have taken any music exams, include the grades achieved). School drama productions. If you have taken the lead, name the play and give dates.

Out of school activities

Sport, music, drama, scouts, guides, youth hostelling, fell walking (give name, dates and places visited). Exchange visits abroad.

Work experience

Details of part-time holiday work, particularly if it relates to the subject of your chosen course. Work observation in hospitals, law courts, business organisations etc. (This is important if you are applying for vocational courses.) If you are applying for a vocational course it could be useful to use this sub-section as the main heading.

Proposed career (if decided)

Unless you are applying for a vocational course there is no need to mention a possible future career which is after all at least four years away!

Finally, photocopy your form for your own reference. If you are interviewed they will probably ask questions about some of the points you have mentioned so – BE HONEST!

9 PRACTICE IN THE EUROPEAN COMMUNITY

In 1985, the European Commission instituted a major new approach to tackle restrictions imposed on the harmonisation of the legal and other professions which would allow those concerned to practise their profession freely within the Community. It put forward a draft directive on higher education diplomas, under which the qualifications necessary to pursue a profession in one Member State would be recognised throughout the Community. The directive applies to all professions to which access is in some way restricted by the state and which require at least three years' university level training or equivalent plus any appropriate job-based training. It will therefore apply to lawyers, accountants, engineers and many others.

The Directive was agreed by the Council of Ministers in December 1988 and Member States were required to have it implemented by 4 January 1991. It enables a professional from one Member State to become a member of the equivalent profession in another Member State without having to requalify.

It does so by introducing the principle of mutual recognition; in other words a fully qualified professional in one Member State is deemed to be fully qualified in another, subject to two safeguards designed to maintain professional standards.

The first involves the length of education and training which the professional has received in their own country. If it is shorter than that required in the country to which they wish to move, the professional concerned may be required to produce evidence of up to four years' experience as a fully qualified professional in another EC country in addition to their professional education and training. This ensures that any shortfall in the length of training is made good by professional experience, thus bringing the person concerned up to an equivalent level of expertise.

The second safeguard takes effect where there is a substantial difference in the content of education and training in a given profession between two EC states. This applies even where the length of the two professional training courses is the same. There are two main reasons why the content of a course might differ substantially. Firstly, the actual boundaries of a profession may vary between Member States. Secondly, the boundaries of a profession may be the same but there may be individual subjects which are specific to one Member State and which are essential in order to operate as a fully qualified professional in that state.

In the above situations, incoming professionals may be required to undergo a test known as the Qualified Lawyers Transfer Test in England and Wales or a period of supervised practice designed to ensure that they have acquired the extra knowledge needed to be a fully effective professional in the field concerned. It comprises either an examination – known as the 'aptitude test' – or a period of assessed supervised practice – known as the 'adaptation period', not exceeding three years, in the country concerned. It is for the incoming professional to choose between the two. The test must not be too difficult and the adaptation period must not be too long.

In some cases an experienced professional who is already familiar with professional requirements in the country to which he or she is applying may choose to take the test. In other cases, a less experienced professional may choose instead to undergo a period of supervised practice with a fully qualified professional from the country concerned in order to adapt to local conditions.

The Directive provides an exception in which the Member State may specify either an aptitude test or an adaptation period for those professions which require a precise knowledge of national law and involve providing advice on national law as a constant and essential aspect of the professional activity.

Now the Directive is in force, all professionals whose qualifications fall within its scope will have a right to have their qualifications recognised in another Member State. To do so, they should first consult the list of 'competent authorities' – bodies responsible for receiving applications to practise in the relevant Member States. Application will be made along with his or her qualifications and the authority will either:

a)   accept the application and grant recognition to the professional concerned, including the right to use the appropriate title or designatory letters;
b)   require the professional to produce evidence of further professional experience;
c)   require the professional to take an aptitude test or undergo a period of supervised practice;
d)   reject the application.

The competent authority's decision must in any case be supported by reasons and the professional will have a right of appeal to a national court or tribunal.

To take advantage of these opportunities, members of the professions will need to be prepared. Languages are an obvious area for attention. English is widely spoken and understood within the Community but knowledge of languages in other Member States will be essential for practising there. A knowledge of the relevant language will be a significant part of the professional's overall marketability.

10 QUALIFYING AT THE BAR IN THE USA

Generally the United States' 'legal market' is open to anyone with basic legal qualifications. Because of the jurisdiction in the 50 different states I have chosen the New York and Californian Bars as examples, in order to demonstrate how the system in America works.

The New York Bar

For the New York Bar, eligibility can only be determined by the New York Board of Law Examiners. It is the responsibility of each applicant to confirm their eligibility with the Board of Examiners. The minimum requirement is a 2:2 degree or its equivalent. The candidate must have completed a three-year law degree in order to sit for the Bar examinations. The applicant must also be over 21 years of age. In order to open up the market the applicant is not required to be a resident of New York State or even a citizen of the United States.

The student must demonstrate that he has completed the degree in a law school approved in the country in which it is located and he must also satisfy the Board of Examiners that the degree that he has studied was based on the English Common Law.

The New York Bar examinations themselves are divided into several parts. The New York portion of the examination is based on procedural and substantive law. In addition candidates must sit for the multi-state Bar examination paper which involves 200 multiple choice questions prepared by the National Conference of Bar Examiners. This part of the examination can be taken in another jurisdiction as it is common to all of the 50 states. The third part of the examination is important; this is the multi-state professional responsibility examination. No applicant can be admitted to the New York Bar without successfully completing all these examinations. The multi-state professional responsibility examination consists of multiple choice questions in the field of professional responsibility but is administered by the National Conference of Bar examiners. The examinations are held three times a year in March, August and November. The examinations are conducted in Albany, the capital of New York State.

On passing the examination the candidate is certified as a member of the New York Bar.

The Californian Bar

The Californian Bar is open to candidates who have at least a 2:2 law degree. There are two categories of applicants in California. These are called 'general applicants' and 'attorney applicants'.

General Applicants

General applicants must be at least 18 years of age and of good moral character. They must have graduated from a college or university approved by the American Bar Association or the Department of Education. Applicants are considered from those with a US law degree, those who have passed the Bar examinations of a sister state in the United States, and also from candidates who have obtained similar qualifications overseas where the Common Law of England constitutes the basis of jurisdiction.

Attorney Applicants

Attorney applications must be from other sister states who wish to be admitted to the Californian Bar. A lawyer who is licensed to practise in a country other than the United States must sit for the General Bar Examination no matter how long the candidate has practised in his or her native country.

The examination consists for four parts:

a)   The Californian State Bar examination which is an essay test.
b)   The Multi-state Bar examination.
c)   The Californian State Bar examination, which unlike the essay test, is a performance test involving drafting, inter-relational skills, negotiation etc.
d)   The Multi-State Professional Responsibility Examination which involves some accounts and ethics.

On successful completion of the examination the applicant is certified as a member of the Californian Bar.

Those candidates who are attorney applicants only need to sit for the Multi-State Professional Responsibility Examination if the pass mark in the state in which they have taken the examination is lower than the pass mark for California.

11 GRADUATE EMPLOYMENT

Graduate employment

There are more misconceptions about graduate employment than any other aspect of higher education. It is generally firmly believed that a degree course must always be a preparation for a certain career, eg Law for the legal profession, English for journalism, French for translating and interpreting and teaching courses for teaching. Nothing could be further from the truth! A four-year degree course of teacher training for example can certainly lead to a satisfying career in the classroom, but it is also an excellent preparation for any job dealing with people, and as the following tables show, some graduates go into business, administration and social work from a range of degree subjects.

A degree or diploma course therefore should be seen as an extension to your education. In some cases it will prepare you for a specific career, but it will also open many other doors.

The tables which follow refer to the types of work which new graduates from the university sector (men and women) entered in 1992.

Table A Type of work of new first degree university graduates entering UK employment – 1992, men and women (per cent).

DEGREE SUBJECT	Scientific/ Eng R&D	Env Planning	Scientific/ Eng Support	Computing	Legal/ information	Creative
Pre-clin medic	0	0	0	0	0	0
Pre-clin dent						
Clinical med	0	0	0	0	0	0
Clinical dent	0	0	0	0	0	0
Anatomy/physio	26	0	9	0	4	1
Pharmacology	40	0	11	0	6	5
Pharmacy	1	0	0	0	0	0
Ophthalmics	0	0	0	0	0	0
Nursing	0	0	0	0	0	0
Biology	26	1	12	3	2	3
Botany	24	0	8	3	3	5
Zoology	18	0	8	2	3	3
Genetics	40	0	13	5	3	0
Microbiology	38	0	33	1	0	2
Biochemistry	37	0	17	3	2	2
Psychology sc	6	0	1	2	2	2
Veterinary sci.	0	0	0	0	0	0
Agriculture	7	2	7	0	0	0
Forestry	3	0	6	3	0	0
Food science	34	0	6	1	0	0
Chemist	30	1	11	4	3	3
Physics	29	0	4	13	2	1
Astronomy	27	0	0	9	0	9
Geology	28	5	7	4	2	2
Geography sci	5	6	3	4	1	2
Maths	5	0	1	15	1	1
Statistics	3	0	1	30	2	0
Computing	12	0	1	68	0	0

This table does not include the percentages of students who, on graduation, entered further training. For example 82 per cent of Law graduates proceed to training as solicitors or barristers or in other careers, eg business, teaching etc.

Social Welfare	Teaching	Admin Management trainee	Financial work	Buying marketing, selling	Clerical/ secretarial
0	0	0	40	40	20
100	0	0	0	0	0
100	0	0	0	0	0
25	0	5	12	4	14
2	0	5	11	10	10
99	0	0	0	0	0
100	0	0	0	0	0
88	10	1	0	0	0
6	2	9	9	11	16
3	0	8	14	14	19
8	3	9	9	8	28
3	0	10	13	5	10
1	0	8	2	12	4
5	1	7	6	9	12
42	4	10	6	8	17
98	1	1	0	0	1
6	0	34	5	17	21
3	0	64	6	3	12
3	0	33	2	9	11
4	2	10	16	8	10
6	1	8	18	6	11
0	0	18	9	0	27
5	1	12	4	4	28
10	3	17	17	13	20
3	2	5	52	5	11
2	1	10	37	8	7
1	1	3	4	3	6

Table B Type of work of new first degree university graduates
entering UK employment – 1992, men and women (per cent).

DEGREE SUBJECT	Scientific/ Eng R&D	Env Planning	Scientific/ Eng Support	Computing	Legal/ information	Creative
Engineering						
General	46	7	1	10	0	1
Civil	10	76	1	0	0	0
Mechanical	71	1	6	2	1	1
Aeronautical	58	1	3	3	1	2
Electrical	56	0	5	20	1	1
Electronic	58	0	7	19	0	0
Electrical/onic	67	0	5	13	0	0
Production	63	1	4	9	0	0
Chemical	75	1	3	1	0	0
Minerals tech.	52	5	11	0	2	0
Metallurgy	50	0	6	2	4	4
Other materials	39	0	14	3	4	2
Maritime tech	88	4	4	0	0	0
Biotechnology	47	0	0	7	0	0
Architecture	1	88	1	0	0	1
Building	9	72	1	0	0	0
Town/c planning	0	55	0	3	1	0
Economics	0	0	0	9	1	1
Sociology	0	0	1	1	5	1
Social policy	2	0	0	2	6	2
Applied social	0	0	0	0	0	0
Anthropology	0	0	0	2	0	9
Psychology SSc	5	0	0	4	1	1
Geography SSc	2	3	1	4	3	1
Politics	0	0	0	1	5	5
Law	1	1	0	2	27	2
Business studies	1	0	1	7	1	1
Financial man	0	0	0	2	0	1
Accountancy	0	0	0	0	0	0

This table does not include the percentages of students who, on graduation, entered
further training. For example 82 per cent of Law graduates proceed to training as
solicitors or barristers or in other careers, eg business, teaching etc.

Social Welfare	Teaching	Admin Management trainee	Financial work	Buying marketing, selling	Clerical/ secretarial
2	6	6	16	4	3
2	0	2	2	2	4
2	0	7	4	2	4
3	0	19	4	1	8
1	1	6	2	2	5
1	0	5	3	3	4
1	0	4	3	2	4
2	0	8	4	6	4
1	0	6	6	3	4
0	0	7	14	0	9
4	2	2	12	10	6
1	0	14	5	14	5
0	0	4	0	0	0
7	0	13	13	7	7
0	0	1	1	1	4
1	0	6	4	4	2
1	0	9	19	1	10
3	0	9	58	9	9
32	10	13	5	11	21
39	6	14	8	3	18
98	2	0	0	0	0
26	9	15	11	15	15
46	6	8	1	9	20
10	2	16	21	14	23
16	1	19	14	14	23
11	6	13	17	5	14
6	1	19	30	25	8
1	0	9	73	6	8
1	0	5	87	2	4

Table C Type of work of new first degree university graduates entering UK employment – 1990, men and women (per cent).

DEGREE SUBJECT	Scientific/ Eng R&D	Env Planning	Scientific/ Eng Support	Computing	Legal/ information	Creative
Instit manag	6	0	1	1	0	0
Land/property	0	6	0	1	1	0
Librarianship	0	0	0	0	78	0
Linguistics		0		0	0	0
English		0		0	0	2
American stds		0		0	0	0
Classical stds		0		0	0	5
French		0		0	0	2
German		1		0	0	2
Hispanic stds		0		2	0	2
Russian		2		0	0	4
Other Euro langs		0		0	0	0
Chinese		0		0	0	8
Other oriental		0		0	0	4
History		0		0	0	2
History of art		0		1	0	1
Archaeology		3		1	0	0
Philosophy		0		0	0	8
Theology		0		0	1	0
Fine art		0		0	2	0
Design studies		14		0	0	0
Music		1		0	1	1
Drama		0		0	0	0
Teacher training		0		0	0	0
Education stds		0		0	0	0

This table does not include the percentages of students who, on graduation, entered further training. For example 82 per cent of Law graduates proceed to training as solicitors or barristers or in other careers, eg business, teaching etc.

Social Welfare	Teaching	Admin Management trainee	Financial work	Buying marketing, selling	Clerical/ secretarial
2	0	61	8	13	10
1	0	19	58	6	8
0	0	11	0	6	6
3	21	9	0	9	9
6	12	10	4	14	8
5	8	7	2	13	2
5	5	14	8	12	21
3	4	4	5	18	16
11	8	6	2	16	17
4	2	9	4	19	19
14	2	10	6	12	12
8	3	6	5	20	14
8	15	0	0	8	15
15	23	12	4	4	15
9	4	10	3	17	17
15	12	8	3	17	4
44	5	9	3	8	6
6	4	22	6	16	12
2	4	62	4	6	2
2	48	4	7	4	4
0	41	8	8	8	0
3	24	11	18	6	6
2	42	7	4	12	0
0	0	3	94	1	0
0	0	11	83	3	0

12 UNIVERSITIES AND COLLEGES

The following is a list of the major higher education institutions in the UK.

Aberdeen (Univ): (*The University of Aberdeen, Regent Walk, Aberdeen AB9 1FX, Scotland. Tel 0224 273504*).

Aberystwyth (Univ): See under Wales (Univ).

Anglia (Poly Univ): (*Anglia Polytechnic University, Cambridge Campus: East Road, Cambridge CB1 1PT. Tel 0223 63271; or Chelmsford Campus: Victoria Road South, Chelmsford, Essex CM1 1LL. Tel 0245 493131*).

Aston (Univ): (*Aston University, Aston Triangle, Birmingham B4 7ET. Tel 021 359 6313*).

Bangor Normal (CHE): (*Bangor Normal College, Bangor, Gwynedd, North Wales LL57 2PX. Tel 0248 370171*).

Bangor (Univ): See under Wales (Univ).

Bath (CHE): (*Bath College of Higher Education, Newton Park, Bath BA2 9BN. Tel 0225 873701*).

Bath (Univ): (*The University of Bath, Claverton Down, Bath BA2 7AY. Tel 0225 826826*).

Bedford (CHE): (*Bedford College of Higher Education, 37 Lansdowne Road, Bedford MK40 2BZ. Tel 0234 351966*).

Belfast (Univ): (*The University of Belfast, University Road, Belfast BT7 1NN, Northern Ireland. Tel 0232 245133*).

Birmingham (Univ): Validates the degrees of Newman & Westhill College, Birmingham. The University is located at Edgbaston, $2^1/_2$ miles from city. (*The University of Birmingham, PO Box 363, Birmingham B15 2TT. Tel 021 414 3344*).

Bishop Grosseteste (CHE): The college offers four-year BEd (Hons) courses awarded by the University of Hull. (*Bishop Grosseteste College, Newport, Lincoln LN1 3DY. Tel 0522 527347*).

Bolton (IHE): (*Bolton Institute of Higher Education, Deane Road, Bolton BL3 5AB. Tel 0204 28851*).

Bournemouth (Univ): (*Bournemouth University, Dorset House, Talbot Campus, Fern Barrow, Dorset BH12 5BB. Tel 0202 595448*).

Bradford (Univ): (*The University, Bradford, West Yorkshire BD7 1DP. Tel 0274 733466*).

Bradford and Ilkley (CmC): (*Bradford and Ilkley Community College, Great Horton Road, Bradford, West Yorkshire BD7 1AY. Tel 0274 733466*).

Bretton Hall (CHE): (*Bretton Hall College, West Bretton, Wakefield, West Yorkshire WF4 4LG. Tel 0924 830261*).

Brighton (Univ): (*University of Brighton, Lewes Road, Brighton BN2 4AT. Tel 0273 600900*).

Bristol (Univ): (*The University of Bristol, Senate House, Bristol BS8 1TH. Tel 0272 303030*).

Bristol (UWE): (*University of the West of England, Bristol, Coldharbour Lane, Frenchay, Bristol BS16 1QY. Tel 0272 656261 – Admissions 0272 763809*).

Brunel (Univ): (*Brunel, The University of West London, Uxbridge, Middlesex UB8 3PH. Tel 0895 274000*).

Buckingham (Univ): (*The University of Buckingham, Hunter Street, Buckingham MK18 1EG. Tel 0280 814080*).

Buckinghamshire (CHE): (*Buckinghamshire College, Queen Alexandra Road, High Wycombe, Buckinghamshire HP11 2JZ. Tel 0494 522141*).

Camborne (School of Mines): (now part of Exeter University) (*Camborne School of Mines, Trevenson, Pool, Redruth, Cornwall TR15 3SE. Tel 0209 714866*).

Cambridge (Univ): There are three colleges which admit women only (Lucy Cavendish – mature women, New Hall and Newnham) and 25 which admit both men and women undergraduates. These are Christ's, Churchill, Clare, Corpus Christi, Downing, Emmanuel, Fitzwilliam, Girton, Gonville & Caius, Homerton (BEd only), Jesus, King's, Magdalene, Pembroke, Peterhouse, Queens', Robinson, St Catharine's, St Edmund's (graduates and mature undergraduates), St John's, Selwyn, Sidney Sussex, Trinity, Trinity Hall and Wolfson. (Enquiries should be addressed to the *Tutor for Admissions, ... College, Cambridge,* or to *Cambridge Intercollegiate Applications Office, Tennis Court Road, Cambridge CB2 1QJ. Tel 0223 333308*).

Canterbury Christ Church (CHE): (*Canterbury Christ Church College of Higher Education, North Holmes Road, Canterbury, Kent CT1 1QU. Tel 0227 762444*).

Cardiff (IHE): (*Cardiff Institute of Higher Education, PO Box 377, Llandaff Centre, Western Avenue, Cardiff CF5 2SG. Tel 0222 551111*).

Cardiff (Univ): See under Wales (Univ).

Central England (Univ): (*University of Central England in Birmingham, Perry Bar, Birmingham B42 2SU. Tel 021 331 5000*).

Central Lancashire (Univ): (*The University of Central Lancashire, Preston PR1 2TQ. Tel 0772 892000*).

Charlotte Mason (CEd): (Degrees validated by Lancaster University) (*Charlotte Mason College of Education, Ambleside, Cumbria LA22 9BB. Tel 05394 33066*).

Cheltenham and Gloucester (CHE): (*Cheltenham and Gloucester College of Higher Education, The Park, Cheltenham, Gloucestershire GL50 2RH. Tel 0242 532824*).

Chester (CHE): (Degrees validated by Liverpool University) (*Chester College, Cheyney Road, Chester CH1 4BJ. Tel 0244 375444*).

City (Univ): (*The City University, Northampton Square, London EC1V OHB. Tel 071 477 8000*).

Colchester (Inst): (*Colchester Institute, Sheepen Road, Colchester CO3 3LL. Tel 0206 761660*).

Coventry (Univ): (*Coventry University, Priory Street, Coventry CV1 5FB. Tel 0203 631313*).

Cranfield (IT): (*Cranfield Institute of Technology, Bedford MK43 0AL. Tel 0234 750111*).

Cranfield (Silsoe): (*Silsoe College, Bedford MK45 4DT. Tel 0525 860428*).

Cranfield (Shrivenham): (*The Royal Military College of Science, Shrivenham, Swindon, Wiltshire SN6 8LA. Tel 0793 785400/1*).

Dartington (CA): (*Dartington College of Arts, Totnes, Devon TQ9 6EJ. Tel 0803 863234*).

De Montfort (Univ): (*De Montfort University, PO Box 143, Leicester LE1 9BH. Tel 0533 551551*).

Derby (Univ): (*University of Derby, Kedleston Road, Derby DE3 1GB. Tel 0332 47181*).

Doncaster (Coll): (*Doncaster College, Waterdale, Doncaster DN1 3EX. Tel 0302 322122*).

Dundee (Univ): (*The University, Dundee, DD1 4HN Scotland. Tel 0382 23181; Admissions: ext 4028*).

Durham-Tees (Coll): (*The Admissions Officer, Joint University College on Teesside, Durham-Tees College, Old Shire Hall, Durham DH1 3HP. Tel 0642 618020*).

Durham (Univ): There are 12 colleges, namely Grey, Hatfield, St Chad's, University, St Mary's, Collingwood, St Aidan's, St Cuthbert's, St Hild/St Bede, St John's, Trevelyan, Van Mildert. All are mixed colleges except St Mary's which is for women only. There is also one society which admits undergraduates. (*The University of Durham, Old Shire Hall, Durham DH1 3HP. Tel 091 374 2000*).

East Anglia (Univ): (*The University of East Anglia, Norwich NR4 7TJ. Tel 0603 56161*).

East London (Univ): (*The University of East London, Romford Road, London E15 4LZ. Tel 081 590 7722*).

Edge Hill (CHE): (*Edge Hill College of Higher Education, St Helen's Road, Ormskirk, Lancashire L39 4QP. Tel 0695 575171*).

Edinburgh (Univ): (*The University, Old College, South Bridge, Edinburgh EH8 9YL, Scotland. Tel 031 650 1000*).

Essex (Univ): (*The University of Essex, Wivenhoe Park, Colchester CO4 3SQ. Tel 0206 873666*).

Exeter (Univ): (*The University, Northcote House, The Queen's Drive, Exeter, Devon EX4 4QJ. Tel 0392 263263*).

Glamorgan (Univ): (*The University of Glamorgan, Pontypridd, Mid-Glamorgan CF37 1DL. Tel 0443 480480*).

Glasgow (Univ): (*The University, Glasgow G12 8QQ, Scotland. Tel 041 339 8855*).

Glasgow Caledonian (Univ): (*Glasgow Caledonian University, 70 Cowcaddens Road, Glasgow G4 0BA. Tel 041 331 3000*).

Greenwich (Univ): (*The University of Greenwich, Wellington Street, London SE18 6PF. Tel 081 316 8590*).

Gwent (CHE): (*Gwent College of Higher Education, College Crescent, Caerleon, Newport, Gwent NP6 1XJ. Tel 0633 432432*).

Heriot-Watt (Univ): (*Heriot-Watt University, Riccarton, Edinburgh EH14 4AS, Scotland. Tel 031 449 5111*).

Hertfordshire (Univ): (*University of Hertfordshire, College Lane, Hatfield, Herts AL10 9AB. Tel 0707 279000*).

Holborn (Coll): (*Holborn College, 200 Greyhound Road, London W14 9RY. Tel 071 385 3377*).

Homerton (Coll): This is an approved society of Cambridge University with 690 students. It offers a Bachelor of Education degree awarded by the University. (*Homerton College, Hills Road, Cambridge. Tel 0223 245931*).

Huddersfield (Univ): (*The University of Huddersfield, Queensgate, Huddersfield HD1 3DH. Tel 0484 422288*).

Hull (Univ): (*The University, Hull, North Humberside HU6 7RX. Tel 0482 46311*).

Humberside (Univ): (*The University of Humberside, Cottingham Road, Hull HU6 7RT. Tel 0482 445005*).

Keele (Univ): (*The University of Keele, Staffordshire ST5 5BG. Tel 0782 621111*).

Kent (Univ): (*The University of Kent at Canterbury, Canterbury, Kent CT2 7NZ. Tel 0227 764000*).

King Alfred's (CHE): (*King Alfred's College, Sparkford Road, Winchester, Hampshire SO22 4NR. Tel 0962 841515*).

Kingston (Univ): (*Kingston University, Penrhyn Road, Kingston upon Thames, Surrey KT1 2EE. Tel 081 547 2000*).

Lancaster (Univ): (*Lancaster Univeristy, University House, Lancaster LA1 4YW. Tel 0524 65201*).

La Sainte Union (CHE): (*La Sainte Union College of Higher Education, The Avenue, Southampton, Hampshire SO9 5HB. Tel 0703 228761*).

Leeds Met (Univ): (*Leeds Metropolitan University, Calverley Street, Leeds LS1 3HE. Tel 0532 832600*).

Leeds (Univ): (*The University of Leeds, Leeds LS2 9JT. Tel 0532 333993*).

Leicester (Univ): (*The University of Leicester, University Road, Leicester LE1 7RH. Tel 0533 522522*).

Liverpool (IHE): Courses are validated by Liverpool University. (*Liverpool Institute of Higher Education, PO Box 6, Stand Park Road, Childwall, Liverpool L16 9JD. Tel 051 737 3000*).

Liverpool John Moores (Univ): (*Liverpool John Moores University, 70 Mount Pleasant, Liverpool L3 5UX. Tel 051 207 3581*).

Liverpool (Univ): (*The University of Liverpool, PO Box 147, Liverpool L69 3BX. Tel 051 794 2000*).

London Guildhall (Univ): (*London Guildhall University, India House, 139 Minories, London EC3N 2EY. Tel 071 320 1000*).

London (Univ) – Courtauld Institute of Art: (*The Courtauld Institute of Art, Somerset House, Strand, London WC2R 0RN. Tel 071 873 2645*).

London (Univ) – Goldsmiths College: (*Goldsmiths College, Lewisham Way, London SE14 6NW. Tel 081 692 7171*).

London (Univ) – Heythrop College: (*Heythrop College, 11-13 Cavendish Square, London W1M 0AN. Tel 071 580 6941*)

London (Univ) – Imperial College of Science, Technology and Medicine: (*Imperial College of Science and Technology, South Kensington, London SW7 2AZ. Tel 071 589 5111*).

London (Univ) – King's College: (*King's College, Strand, London WC2R 2LS. Tel 071 836 5454*).

London (Univ) – Queen Mary and Westfield College: (*Queen Mary College, Mile End Road, London E1 4NS. Tel 071 975 5555*).

London (Univ) – Royal Holloway: (*Royal Holloway, Egham Hill, Egham, Surrey TW20 0EX. Tel 0784 434455*).

London (Univ) – Royal Veterinary College: (*Royal Veterinary College, Royal College Street, London NW1 0TU. Tel 071 387 2898*).

London (Univ) – School of Economics and Political Science (LSE): (*London School of Economics and Political Science, Houghton Street, Aldwych, London WC2A 2AE. Tel 071 405 7686*).

London (Univ) – School of Oriental and African Studies (SOAS): (*The School of Oriental and African Studies, Thornhaugh Street, Russell Square, London WC1M 0XG. Tel 071 637 2388*).

London (Univ) – School of Pharmacy: (*The School of Pharmacy, 29-39 Brunswick Square, London WC1N 1AX. Tel 071 753 5800*).

London (Univ) – School of Slavonic and East European Studies (SSEES): (*The School of Slavonic and East European Studies, Malet Street, London WC1E 7HU. Tel 071 637 4934*).

London (Univ) – University College: (*University College, Gower Street, London WC1E 6BT. Tel 071 387 7050*).

London (Univ) – Wye: (*Wye College, Wye, Ashford, Kent TN25 5AH. Tel 0233 812401*).

London Medical and Dental Schools

Charing Cross and Westminster Medical School St Dunstan's Road, London W6 8RP. Tel 081 846 7272.

King's College Hospital School of Medicine and Dentistry Bessemer Road, London SE5 9PJ. Tel 071 274 6222; Dental School Tel 071 326 3079.

London Hospital Medical College (Dentistry and Medicine) Turner Street, London E1 2AD. Tel 071 377 7611.

Royal Free Hospital School of Medicine Rowland Hill Street, London NW3 2PF. Tel 071 794 0500.

St Bartholomew's Hospital Medical College (Dentistry and Medicine) West Smithfield, London EC1A 7BE. Tel 071 601 8834.

St George's Hospital Medical School Cranmer Terrace, Tooting, London SW17 0RE. Tel 081 672 9944.

St Mary's Hospital Medical School Norfolk Place, Paddington, London W2 1PG. Tel 071 723 1252.

United Medical and Dental Schools of Guy's and St Thomas's Hospitals (Dentistry and Medicine) St Thomas's Campus, Lambeth Palace Road, London SE1 7EH. Tel 071 922 8013.

University College and Middlesex School of Medicine, University College London Gower Street, London WC1 6JJ. Tel 071 387 7050.

Loughborough (Univ): (*University of Technology, Loughborough, Leicester LE11 3TU. Tel 0509 263171*).

Luton: (*Luton University, Park Square, Luton, Bedfordshire LU1 3JU. Tel 0582 34111*).

Manchester Met (Univ): (*Manchester Metropolitan University, All Saints, Manchester M15 6BH. Tel 061 247 2000*).

Manchester (Univ): (*The University of Manchester, Manchester M13 9PL. Tel 061 275 2000*).

Manchester – The University of Manchester Institute of Science and Technology (UMIST): (*The University of Manchester Institute of Science and Technology, Manchester M60 1QD. Tel 061 236 3311*).

Matthew Boulton (CFHE): (*Matthew Boulton College of Further and Higher Education, Sherlock Street, Birmingham B5 7DB. Tel 021 446 4545*).

Middlesex (Univ): (*Middlesex University, Bramley Road, Oakwood, London N14 4XS. Tel 081 368 1299*).

Napier (Univ): (*Napier University of Edinburgh, 219 Colinton Road, Edinburgh EH14 1DJ. Tel 031 444 2266*).

Nene (CHE): (*Nene College, Moulton Park, Northampton NN2 7AL. Tel 0604 735500*).

New College, Durham: (*New College, Framwellgate Moor Centre, Durham DH1 5ES. Tel 091 386 2421*).

Newcastle (Univ): (*The University of Newcastle upon Tyne, 6 Kensington Terrace, Newcastle upon Tyne, NE1 7RU. Tel 091 222 6000*).

Newman and Westhill (CHE): Courses are validated by Birmingham University. (*Newman College, Genners Lane, Bartley Green, Birmingham B32 3NT. Tel 021 476 1181; Westhill College, Weoley Park Road, Selly Oak, Birmingham B29 6LL. Tel 021 472 7245*).

North Cheshire (CHE): (*North Cheshire College, Padgate Campus, Fearnhead, Warrington WA2 0DB. Tel 0925 814343*).

Nescot (CT): (*Nescot, Reigate Road, Ewell, Epsom, Surrey KT17 3DS. Tel 081 394 1731*).

North East Wales (IHE): (*North East Wales Institute of Higher Education, Cartrefle, Mold Road, Wrexham, Clwyd LL11 2AW. Tel 0978 290666*).

North London (Univ): (*The University of North London, Holloway Road, London N7 8DB. Tel 071 607 2789*).

North Riding (Coll): Courses are validated by Leeds University. (*North Riding College, Filey Road, Scarborough, North Yorkshire YO11 3AZ. Tel 0723 362392*).

Northumbria (Univ): (*The University of Northumbria at Newcastle, Ellison Place, Newcastle upon Tyne NE1 8ST. Tel 091 232 6002*).

Nottingham Trent (Univ): (*Nottingham Trent University, Burton Street, Nottingham NG1 4BU. Tel 0602 418418*).

Nottingham (Univ): (*The University of Nottingham, University Park, Nottingham NG7 2RD. Tel 0602 484848*).

Oxford Brookes (Univ): (*Oxford Brookes University, Headington, Oxford OX3 0BP. Tel 0865 741111*).

Oxford (Univ): 35 colleges admitting students (M) = Men only; (W) = Women only. All other colleges are mixed. *Group 1*: Brasenose, Christ Church, Jesus, Lincoln, Magdalen, Merton, Oriel, St Hilda's (W), Somerville; *Group 2*: Balliol, Exeter, Keble, Pembroke, St Anne's, St Edmund Hall, St John's, St Peter's, Wadham; *Group 3*: Corpus Christi, Hertford, Lady Margaret Hall, New College, Queen's, St Catherine's, St Hugh's, Trinity, University, Worcester. *Private Halls*: Campion Hall (M), St Benet's Hall (M), Mansfield, Regent's Park, Greyfriars (M). (Enquiries should be addressed to *The Tutor for .... Admissions, ... College, Oxford*, or *The Oxford Colleges Admissions Office, University Offices, Wellington Square, Oxford OX1 2JD. Tel 0865 270207*).

Paisley (Univ): (*Paisley University, High Street, Paisley, Renfrewshire PA1 2BE. Tel 041 848 3000*).

Plymouth (Univ): (*University of Plymouth, Drake Circus, Plymouth PL4 8AA. Tel 0752 600600*).

Portsmouth (Univ): (*The University of Portsmouth, Museum Road, Portsmouth PO1 2QQ. Tel 0705 827681*).

Reading (Univ): (*The University of Reading, PO Box 217, Reading, Berkshire RG6 2AH. Tel 0734 875123*).

Ripon and York St John (CHE): The College offers Leeds University degrees. (*College of Ripon and York St John, Lord Mayor's Walk, York YO3 7EX. Tel 0904 656771*).

Robert Gordon (Univ): (*Robert Gordon University, Schoolhill, Aberdeen AB9 1FR. Tel 0224 633611*).

Roehampton (IHE): The Institute offers Surrey University single and joint honours degrees. (*Roehampton Institute, Roehampton Lane, London SW15 5PU. Tel 081 878 8117*).

St Andrews (Univ): (*The University of St Andrews, College Gate, St Andrews, Fife KY16 9AJ. Tel 0334 76161*).

St David's (Univ): See under Wales (Univ)

St Mark and St John (CHE): Degrees are validated by Exeter University. (*St Mark and St John College, Derriford Road, Plymouth PL6 8BH. Tel 0752 777188*).

St Martin's (CHE): (*St Martin's College, Lancaster LA1 3JD. Tel 0524 63446*).

St Mary's (CHE): The college offers degrees awarded by Surrey University. (*St Mary's College, Strawberry Hill, Twickenham, Middlesex TW1 4SX. Tel 081 892 0051*).

Salford (Univ): (*The University of Salford, Salford M5 4WT. Tel 061 745 5000*).

Salford (Univ Coll): (*Salford University College, Frederick Road, Salford M6 6PU. Tel 061 736 6541*).

Sheffield (Univ): (*The University of Sheffield, Western Bank, Sheffield S10 2TN. Tel 0742 768555*). Medical School. *Tel 0742 766222*.

Sheffield Hallam (Univ): (*Sheffield Hallam University, Pond Street, Sheffield S1 1WB. Tel 0742 720911*).

Southampton (IHE): Degree courses validated by Southampton University. (*Southampton Institute of Higher Education, East Park Terrace, Southampton SO9 4WW. Tel 0703 229381*).

Southampton (Univ): (*The University of Southampton, Highfield, Southampton SO9 5NH. Tel 0703 595000*).

South Bank (Univ): (*South Bank University, Borough Road, London SE1 0AA. Tel 071 928 8989*).

South Devon (CAT): (*South Devon College of Arts and Technology, Newton Road, Torquay, Devon. Tel 0803 213242*).

Staffordshire (Univ): (*Staffordshire University, College Road, Stoke-on-Trent ST4 2DE. Tel 0785 52331*).

Stirling (Univ): (*The University of Stirling, Stirling FK9 4LA, Scotland. Tel 0786 73171*).

Strathclyde (Univ): (*The University of Strathclyde, 16 Richmond Street, Glasgow G1 1XQ, Scotland. Tel 041 553 4170*).

Suffolk (CFHE): (*Suffolk College, Rope Walk, Ipswich, Suffolk. Tel 0473 255885*).

Sunderland (Univ): (*University of Sunderland, Ryhope Road, Sunderland, Tyne and Wear SR2 7EE. Tel 091 515 2000*).

Surrey (Univ): (*The University of Surrey, Guildford, Surrey GU2 5XH. Tel 0483 300800*).

Sussex (Univ): (*The University of Sussex, Sussex House, Falmer, Brighton BN1 9RH. Tel 0273 678416*).

Swansea (IHE): (*Swansea Institute of Higher Education, Townhill Road, Swansea SA2 0UT. Tel 0792 203482*).

Swansea (Univ): See under Wales (Univ).

Teesside (Univ): (*University of Teesside, Borough Road, Middlesbrough, Cleveland TS1 3BA. Tel 0642 218121*).

Thames Valley London (Univ): (*Thames Valley London University, St Mary's Road, London W5 5RF. Tel 081 579 5000*).

Trinity and All Saints (CHE): Courses are validated by Leeds University. (*Trinity and All Saints' College, Brownberrie Lane, Horsforth, Leeds LS18 5HD. Tel 0532 584341*).

Trinity Carmarthen (CHE): (*Trinity College, Carmarthen, Dyfed, South Wales SA31 3EP. Tel 0267 237971*).

Ulster (Univ): (*The University of Ulster, Coleraine, County Londonderry BT52 1SA, Northern Ireland. Tel 0265 44141*).

Wales (Univ) – Aberystwyth: (*The University of Wales, PO Box 2, Aberystwyth, Dyfed SY23 2AX. Tel 0970 622021*).

Wales (Univ) – Bangor: (*The University College of North Wales, Bangor, Gwynedd LL57 2DG. Tel 0248 351151*).

Wales (Univ) – Cardiff: (*The University of Wales College of Cardiff, PO Box 68, Cardiff CF1 3XA. Tel 0222 874412*).

Wales (Univ) – St David's: (*St David's University College, Lampeter, Dyfed SA48 7ED. Tel 0570 422351*).

Wales (Univ) – Swansea: (*University College of Swansea, Singleton Park, Swansea SA2 8PP. Tel 0792 205678*).

Wales (Univ) – College of Medicine (UWCM): (*The University of Wales College of Medicine, Heath Park, Cardiff CF4 4XN. Tel 0222 747747*).

Warwick (Univ): (*The University of Warwick, Coventry CV4 7AL. Tel 0203 523523*).

West Herts (Coll): (*West Hertfordshire College, Hempstead Road, Watford, Hertfordshire WD1 3EZ. Tel 0923 57500*).

West London (IHE): (*West London Institute of Higher Education, 300 St Margarets Road, Twickenham, Middlesex TW1 1FT. Tel 081 891 0121*).

Westminster (CHE): Degrees are validated by Oxford University. (*Westminster College, North Hinksey, Oxford OX2 9AT. Tel 0865 247644*).

Westminster (Univ): (*University of Westminster, 309 Regent Street, London W1R 8AL. Tel 071 911 5000*).

West Sussex (IHE): (*West Sussex Institute of Higher Education, Upper Bognor Road, Bognor Regis, West Sussex PO21 1HR. Tel 0243 865581*).

Wolverhampton (Univ): (*The University of Wolverhampton, Wulfruna Street, Wolverhampton WV1 1SB. Tel 0902 321000*).

Worcester (CHE): (*Worcester College of Higher Education, Henwick Grove, Worcester WR2 6AJ. Tel 0905 748080*).

York (Univ): (*The University of York, Heslington, York YO1 5DD. Tel 0904 430000*).